Faith and Public Policy

Faith and Public Policy

Edited by
James R. Wilburn

LEXINGTON BOOKS
Lanham • Boulder • New York • Oxford

LEXINGTON BOOKS

Published in the United States of America
by Lexington Books
A Member of the Rowman & Littlefield Publishing Group
4720 Boston Way, Lanham, Maryland 20706

PO Box 317
Oxford
OX2 9RU, UK

British Library Cataloguing in Publication Information Available

Library of Congress Cataloging-in-Publication Data

Faith and public policy / edited by James R. Wilburn.
    p. cm.
    Includes bibliographical references and index.
    ISBN 0-7391-0385-7 (alk. paper)—ISBN 0-7391-0386-5 (pbk. : alk. paper)
    1. Christianity and politics—United States—Congresses. I. Wilburn, James R., 1932–

BR526 .F3 2002
261.7'0973—dc21

                                                                2002022234

Printed in the United States of America

♾™ The paper used in this publication meets the minimum requirements of American
National Standard for Information Sciences—Permanence of Paper for Printed Library
Materials, ANSI/NISO Z39.48–1992.

To William E. Simon Sr.,
for inspiring young leaders at
Pepperdine University School of Public Policy

Contents

Acknowledgments

No one has been more instrumental in making possible the annual conferences on Faith and Public Policy on which this collection is based than William E. Simon Sr., Jim and Vicki Click, Gerald and Lucille Isom, and Gerald and Margaret Sheppard. Jim and Vicki were especially helpful in providing early support for preparing the material for publication.

Unfortunately, Bill Simon's untimely death came before he could see the final results of his encouragement. It is altogether fitting that the book should be dedicated to him and his early belief in what the new School of Public Policy at Pepperdine University is attempting to accomplish. His encouragement came in the form of early morning calls from many places on earth as well as from his own personal resources and his leadership at the John M. Olin Foundation, which has played a significant role in the school's founding.

A host of others have helped financially in support of each of the first four annual conferences. We have expressed thanks to them in our printed programs each year, and my appreciation for each of them is no less genuine for my not attempting to list them all here.

As editor, I join the thirteen other authors in expressing appreciation to the people who invested many hours of their lives in seeing the project to its conclusion. As is often the case with publications, just when it seemed that the task was almost complete, another mountaintop emerged over the horizon presenting yet another series of late nights and delayed vacations.

I am especially indebted to Sheryl Kelo, executive program director for the Pepperdine School of Public Policy, for serving as the project manager for all details of preparing the manuscript for the publisher. Joining her has been my assistant, Tami McKelvy, who prepared the first draft of each chapter and then patiently sat down again to deal with the endless revisions that over the course of many months came out of my office to land on her desk. Ms. Kelo prepared the manuscript in final form for the publisher and worked closely with the publisher on various and innumerable details related to the publication.

Assisting Ms. Kelo and Ms. McKelvy in preparing the manuscript and checking numerous details for accuracy has been an army of aides including Kenya Hudson, Ryan Maguire, Aaron Pankratz, Jason Ross, and Jeremy Stewart, Pepperdine University graduate assistants, and Nancy Alvarado. Marie

Lindgren, who has assisted me for more than two decades with numerous publications, copy edited the manuscript, and made invaluable suggestions. Jon Kemp, assistant dean of the School of Public Policy, planned and executed the last two conferences and the leaders whose work appears in the following pages reflect his creative ideas and careful selection of topics and speakers. Serena Leigh has been in charge of all details at Rowman and Littlefield and has provided patient assistance and persisting belief in the project from the beginning.

Both David Davenport, former president of Pepperdine University, and the newly inaugurated president, Andrew K. Benton, have been supportive of the school and particularly of the Faith and Public Policy series. I could not have asked for anyone to be more ready to lend a hand or provide resources when needed.

When I met my wife, Gail, on the Amazon River, I was wrestling with whether to accept the request that I start yet one more new program at Pepperdine University. Since I agreed to serve as the inaugural dean of the new School of Public Policy and she agreed to become my wife, she has been my most steadfast partner in every detail of the entire undertaking. I would not have wanted to do it at all without her help.

I hope that the thoughts and insights of such an incredibly outstanding collection of writers on such a timely topic will contribute significantly to the important conversation currently taking place in our nation about the proper role of faith in the public square.

Introduction

James R. Wilburn

The deep personal faith that informs and fuels the public leadership of some of America's leading thinkers and activists is reflected in the essays that follow. They combine the courage to face the reality of dark forces that challenge our better national instincts with a vibrant hope for the future of the public square. The essays are taken from the first three years of an annual conference on Faith and Public Policy hosted by the new School of Public Policy at Pepperdine University to signal its unique mission.

Faith was an indispensable ingredient in the providential intersection between world forces, gifted leaders, and once-in-a-millennium opportunities that produced the United States of America. Amid much struggle for direction and identity it remains a unique experiment in the history of human culture. Its canon of founding documents clearly demonstrates an enlightened reliance on divine guidance and a clear sense that something very special was being created on the earth.

The first essay underscores the spiritual consequences of certain public policies that are treated in greater detail in subsequent chapters. It also acknowledges that while there is a transcendent purpose evident in the affairs of state, there is also the gravity of individual freedom which places in the hands of each citizen the terrible responsibility of choosing whether to yield to the potential of that larger purpose.

The essays by California Senator Jack Scott and philosopher and theologian Michael Novak elucidate the inseparable relationship between religion and democracy. Scott shows how the strong religious assumptions of the Constitution and the Declaration of Independence embrace the concept of natural law through reason and revelation. These assumptions remain essential two centuries later as religious freedom, as understood in the founding principles, becomes more important rather than less in a society becoming more religiously plural.

Michael Novak adds to these elements of faith and reason the idea of a nation in covenant with God, a dominant theme in the Declaration. Though not all the founders were religious men, the Declaration of Independence contains biblical paradigms: the world had a beginning; it was created purposefully, not accidentally; and Providence, or an intelligent and gracious purpose, was bestowed upon the cosmos placing human liberty in a holy light. More than a Lockean document of self-interest, the Declaration signaled a change from monarchy to a republic, where self-mastery required higher virtues than in a monarchy. Policies often consigned to the state were rather the responsibility of the people and their associations. Instead of understanding religion and government as mutually exclusive spheres, the founders reconciled them.

Thus, as Jean Bethke Elshtain acknowledges, though government and religion in America are less intermingled than in previous cultures, they are inextricably commingled. But she recalls that even Tocqueville in the early nineteenth century understood that there are dangers in this, notably the potential of schism and the temptation to indifference. The danger of schism warns us that differences, if not honored and respected, can become an occasion for isolation which could destroy the rare opportunity we enjoy to be both American and, at the same time, Protestant, Catholic, Jew, or Muslim.

But more dangerous, for professor Elshtain, is the temptation to become indifferent. And apathy can eat away in ways that are no less deadly just because they are subtle. Settling for a smorgasbord of religiosity can make us feel good about ourselves without placing demands on us, a kind of cheap grace. Further, religious institutions themselves can become hollowed out, ceasing to be the carriers of an energetic and authentic faith. Finally, there is the overt curtailment of religion, especially in public spaces, in the name of religious freedom. Ironically, as Americans grow increasingly fearful of religious intolerance, their response is too often to so privatize expressions of faith that they remove religion entirely from the public sphere.

In an attempt to place the conversation on a less sectarian level, James Q. Wilson reminds us that the primary effect of religion is not so much to require obedience to a moral code as to transform lives by understanding ourselves through God. These transformations intersect public policy in various ways, including such clear demonstrations as how religious adherence among black urban youth is inversely related to criminality or the success of faith-based ministries such as Alcoholics Anonymous and prison ministries. He also notes that the First Amendment of the Constitution does not preclude the government from relying on the transformative power of religion, but rather guarantees religious conscience and prevents the government from imposing religious practices. There is no substantial evidence that the framers ever intended to ban nondiscriminatory aid to all religions generally, though there is the potential that federal money can bring federal rules that harm, distort, and burden them.

Wilson notes that of almost sixty billion dollars given annually by Americans to religious groups, little comes from corporations even though they are generous in giving to secular organizations. He proposes a creative plan for a kind of faith-based approximation to the United Way—an independent organization that identifies useful faith-based outreach programs aimed at the kinds of personal conduct such as alcoholism, crime, delinquency, drug abuse, and single-mother pregnancies that concern Americans—to encourage greater corporate support.

Focusing on the charitable choice provisions of the 1996 Welfare Reform Act, Stephen V. Monsma traces an emerging shift away from the debate over more government or less government toward a growing recognition of the essential role that civil society should play in public policy. Closely following this is the recognition that the majority of the private, civil society, health, and social service agencies are nurtured by faith. And such faith, we have come to appreciate, is not incidental, but primary to many social problems plaguing our society as we enter the twenty-first century.

The old paradigm's assumption that secular and religious aspects of a faith-based agency can be neatly separated without hindering its effectiveness has at least three problems. First, it excludes some of the most effective programs since they are religious in nature. Second, when religious aspects of a program must be minimized or compromised, the program's efficacy often is greatly reduced. Third, it discriminates against religion, putting faith-based agencies at a disadvantage compared to their secular counterparts. Charitable choice seeks to return faith-based organizations to their proper role in the civil society while protecting their religious integrity and the religious freedom of the needy whom they serve.

To demonstrate the efficacy of faith-based programs, John J. DiIulio Jr. focuses more closely on the efficacy of such programs among inner-city youth. He reminds us that inner-city children who are most severely at risk deserve to be sheltered—physically, socially, economically, and morally—as they grow toward adulthood. Public–private alliances as well as religious and secular partnerships are necessary to mobilize the human and financial resources that can assure their safety and support. To be more specific, he notes from empirical data from studies in Boston, Philadelphia, and other metropolitan areas that faith-based outreach programs do more and do it better than secular programs alone.

DiIulio concludes that the successful programs he has studied seem to share certain common characteristics. First, religious volunteers lovingly but firmly articulate and enforce a code of conduct. Second, their volunteers are based in the neighborhoods they serve. Third, they are available when the children need them most, when crises erupt. Fourth, they provide an environment free from physical violence or sexual predation. Fifth, they insist on courteous and respectful behavior. Sixth, they require everyone to contribute, sharing leadership and chores. And last, they are places of activity, serving mostly individuals who are not themselves members of the sponsoring organizations. But throughout these observations it is consistently clear that faith is the foundation of their efficacy.

Eloise Anderson, drawing on her broad background in faith-based programs in small churches as well as her responsibilities for two of the largest welfare programs in the nation, first in Michigan and then in California, sounds a convincing note of warning that faith-based programs can very easily become secularized. She maintains that even without formal charitable choice provisions, several larger faith-based social service organizations have become secularized as their attempts to borrow modern management techniques from the corporate world or to take advantage of government or corporate funding can easily take priority over the mission that initially enabled their success. In this she expands on the earlier warning of James Q. Wilson that there is the potential that federal money can bring federal rules that harm, distort, and burden religious institutions, large and small.

Anderson identifies four causes of secularization. As faith-based organizations receive a smaller proportion of their funds from cash and in-kind donations from individuals, they deal less and less with the poor and instead with more diverse interests. The professional trend toward requiring formal training and credentialing from secular agencies attracts personnel whose training and outlook is increasingly more secular than personnel originally attracted to the faith basis of the organization. Simultaneously, as leaders of faith-based social service organizations follow a model of corporate business management, they focus less on the services they provide and more on ensuring the survival of their organization. Finally, government regulations and grant requirements tend to destroy the unique and robust niches of small organizations by requiring that they compete with larger groups for funding, producing a homogenizing effect that compels groups to shape their programs similarly in order to win grants. The combined influence of these strong forces tends, over time, to secularize faith-based groups in spite of their early best intentions.

Shifting from the role of government to the role of the family, Patrick Fagan argues that many of the social ills afflicting children stem from their relationships with their parents and with the relationship their parents have with each other. He marshals an enormous body of social science data to buttress these insights with numerous quantitative exhibits. Girls who are close to their fathers, for instance, tend to remain virgins longer. Childhood poverty is lowest in first families and lower in step-families than in families with merely cohabiting parents or single parents. Child abuse is lowest in intact families that include the biological mother and father. The most dangerous environment for a child, in terms of child abuse, is the home of a single mother with a live-in boyfriend.

Juvenile crime is also closely linked to family structure. Faith plays an important role in forestalling teenage sex and crime. Young men who go to church frequently are less likely to commit crime than those who do not. Fagan's study also reveals that frequent church attendance is linked with the propensity to remain virgins among young men and, to a larger degree, among young women. Data show that regardless of denomination or geography, there are two major factors explaining what is happening to American children who are most successful. These are whether the mother and father who conceived them are together to rear them and whether they worship God in a regular faith community.

Douglas W. Kmiec and Charles Van Eaton both discuss how public policy impacts the ability of families to fulfill their responsibilities. While Fagan demonstrates how the family is critical to public policy in dealing with the social problems that threaten to undermine our free society, Kmiec adds that the family's role extends far beyond its own household since it is the family's primary responsibility to provide for both the intellectual and the moral education of the children who will determine whether democracy survives.

At the heart of the school choice debate is the idea that schools chosen by parents, especially religious schools, become an extension of the family and its values whereas public schools are all too often extensions of government and other interests which may even be contrary to those of the family. Federal public policy as far back as the 1787 Northwest Ordinance has recognized the importance of moral development in education. Yet families are often separated from education because of the Supreme Court's difficulty in reconciling the constitutional provision barring the establishment of religion with religion's obvious connection to the type of moral instruction that must occur in school if it is faithfully to be an extension or teaching agent of parents.

Undeniably, religious schools have shown themselves to be at least as competent and usually more competent than public schools in educational achievement, moral formation, and maintaining safe educational environments. Clearly, there is less violence in religious schools than in public schools. But in addition, studies of the Milwaukee and Ohio choice programs showed higher math and reading scores and higher retention rates for inner-city youth. Religious schools often do this with fewer dollars (in one state, thirty-five hundred versus ten thousand dollars per student). Student achievement is obviously less related to what is spent on education than the existence of a nurturing religious community which ties family and school together.

Part of the current policy challenge to the family is the degree to which public resources are taxed away from the family and directed toward a single education provider. However, Charles Van Eaton calls attention to two other dimensions of federal policy that adversely affect American families. First, the growth of the welfare state has changed our culture's view of the family and its responsibilities. Secondly, the federal income tax has forced both parents in many families to work outside the home, reducing the time available for the daily care and nurture of children. The failure since 1948 to adjust the personal exemption rate in line with inflation has caused a dramatic real decline in disposable family income. In addition, though not intentional, Social Security has weakened the cross-generational obligations that once characterized American families.

As Fagan demonstrates, changing family structure is strongly correlated to increased crime, poverty, educational dysfunction, and other social ills. But Van Eaton maintains that current understandings of the nature of the family itself as a malleable social construction—a thing that can simply be whatever its members want it to be—do not comport with the traditional view of the family found in the Judeo-Christian tradition that sees family as prior to both society and the state. Family members have duties to each other as well as to the family.

Before the 1996 reforms, the welfare system subsidized behavior that created dysfunctional families. To ameliorate at least some of these ills, changes in the welfare system should be expanded to include the elimination of the bias against marriage and children in our tax system.

Having traced the roots of our institutions of government to faith in a transcendent power and having noted the role of faith-based organizations and the family, the final three essays focus on the individual citizen. Not only can one solitary person make a difference, it is ultimately the only way a difference can be made.

Alan Wolfe examines the current relationship between moral freedom and private virtue. He considers four specific virtues—honesty, loyalty, self-discipline, and forgiveness—based on interviews with more than two-hundred Americans. He concludes that the language of virtue has not so much been lost as it is in competition with other values such as mobility, freedom, and the increased medicalization of issues previously described as vices.

He finds that Americans believe in honesty, but a qualified honesty that is not unnecessarily cruel. Further, they believe that it is more important to be honest with family and friends than with strangers and large organizations. Americans also believe that loyalty is important. Yet they observe that disloyalty, in the labor market or among sports franchises threatening to move to other cities, is also rewarded. It is most evident in the startling number of divorces, one of the most wrenching forms of disloyalty. Third, Americans honor self-discipline and the need to delay gratification, but apparently for greater gratification in the future rather than as a self-discipline that is constant over time as its own reward. When persons appear unable to exercise self-discipline, our society tends to medicalize their behavior rather than diagnose it as a character flaw. Finally, Wolfe suggests that forgiveness is a forgotten virtue, certainly the least talked about of the four virtues he examines.

Wolfe concludes that Americans are in a period of adjustment in which they are trying to fit a code of conduct to the notion that they are in charge of their own destinies. He hopes that this transition may lead to greater morality as people feel more responsible for their choices.

Whether or not this optimism is justified, Steve Forbes concludes where the series began—that America's top priority should be understanding that without a moral foundation, freedom leads inevitably to an explosion of moral pathologies and opens the door to tyranny. This truth is no longer self-evident to many Americans, especially among many elites who see religion as little more than a hobby.

However, this is not the first time that America has faced difficulties and overcome them. Rampant alcoholism led to the Great Awakening of the 1820s and the subsequent temperance movement. Teddy Roosevelt used the "bully pulpit" to restore national confidence and reassert the notion that there must be a moral foundation to a free society.

Today, the end of the Cold War presents a unique opportunity to return power and control to families and communities. The dawn of the Information Age has also given individuals more choice and control over their daily lives. These changes are affecting public policy most obviously in the case of welfare reform but have the potential to empower individuals and the mediating institutions which formerly gave such strength to our way of life.

But Forbes urges that we can do more. We can reinforce the importance of marriage. We can overhaul and simplify the tax code to allow struggling families to keep more of what they earn. We can reform adoption laws. We can reject preferential policies so that Americans can begin life as individuals and not as members of groups. We can fight an effective, relentless war against illegal drugs. And, Forbes advocates, we can outlaw partial-birth abortion.

While Forbes calls for another Great Awakening, William E. Simon Sr. intertwines his personal story of the transformative character of faith with a discussion of the role of religion in public policy. Although, as John Adams stated, a moral people is essential to the effectiveness of self-government, and later observers like Tocqueville deemed the piety of Americans as crucial to the American democratic experiment, the past century has seen an attempt to remove faith from the public square and make it wholly a private matter. Examples include the 1962 Supreme Court decision banning prayer in public schools, the annual attempts by the ACLU to remove nativity and other religious displays from public buildings or property, and the difficulty experienced by many faith-based organizations in cutting through regulatory red tape to assist persons in need. The paradox is that this attempt to sever the religious from the public comes at a time when empirical data and anecdotal studies make clear the transformative impact that faith has in ameliorating social ills.

Simon draws heavily from many of his charitable experiences to illustrate that point, including his work as a lay communicant in ministering to terminally ill AIDS patients. Simon's witness, given near the end of his life, is a powerful testimony to the ability of an individual citizen of faith to create a moral climate in which free institutions are most likely to survive and grow.

Chapter 1

Public Policy and Spiritual Consequences

James R. Wilburn

Richard Weaver has reminded us that "ideas have consequences."[1] Indeed, there is no such thing as an inert idea. Powerful ideas of substance hold in their seed form the full potential to alter history, characterize an entire century, or change the way a whole people view the world. Indeed, a single idea can become a touchstone for how the world comes to define what is real and what is illusory.

It is equally true that public policies have consequences. All are aware of their power to alter our lives in significant ways and to erect new categories which constrain or liberate whole nations. But what is seldom appreciated is that these consequences are not limited merely to political, economic, and intellectual outcomes. Public policies affect the whole fabric of life because they are based on certain assumptions about human nature, the purpose of life, and a hierarchy of values. In a word, public policies are ultimately rooted in transcendent commitments and have fundamental spiritual consequences.

That the Founding Fathers of these United States based their decisions on religious precepts is too evident to be disputed. That their political, policy, and legal decisions had spiritual consequences for the institutions of our civilization and the course of our history is also indisputable.

To be sure, theirs was not an intended theocracy. They coveted the importance of their faith too deeply to entrust it to institutions of government and initiated in the First Amendment to the Constitution a bold new experiment in human history which led eventually to the separation of church and state, for the greater integrity and purity of both. The First Amendment was aimed at the federal level to protect the free exercise of personal faith. But within another two decades, the church had been disestablished in Virginia and Massachusetts to confirm and complete the unique separation at the state level.

It was not their intent, nor is it ours today, to suggest that God has blessed a particular form of human political organization as his chosen tabernacle. No human institution can with impunity claim to be ultimate. "Thou shalt have no other gods before me" not only forbids theocracy. It demands a self-questioning

1

humility about our most closely held beliefs, an innocent openness born of a spirit of waiting for further understanding, aware that we are fallible children in a lifelong search for the will of God. Fundamental to the self-renewal of democracy, as for persons, is its willingness to question and purify its beliefs in the fire of investigation.

Public Policy and Religious Assumptions

Having said this, we must acknowledge that embedded in public policy are certain assumptions which are clearly spiritual in nature. And while there may always be some cause for distinguishing between organized religious institutions on the one hand and the spiritual dimension of the human predicament on the other, religion at its best, certainly since the Old Testament prophets, has been wedded not to magic but to a moral journey, not to a place but a state of the heart. In its purest form it is tied closely to our yearnings to be ethical and moral beings, conformed to the character of a just and merciful Creator.

Human Nature

Human nature is a case in point. The Founding Fathers built into the Constitution a balance of powers between branches of government because they were suspicious of our ability to resist the corruption of centralized and absolute power. This reflected not only their own experience, but their careful reading of human history as well. Powerful institutions, whether sacred or secular, have always been seductive magnets, attracting individuals with large egos bent on finding the levers of power with which to impose their intentions on less prideful common folk. But the structure they pursued also reflected religious beliefs expressed powerfully in the Scriptures. One cannot study closely the first eleven chapters of Genesis without coming to understand that for all our lofty accomplishments when we are answering our better angels, the strong inclination of the human race throughout its history has been to be selfish and proud—for men and women to choose their own way in spite of its impact on others. Much debate today over conflicting solutions to policy challenges is, at its deepest and often unseen level, a debate over the true nature of humans. Failure to settle this conflict in the ocean depth of our souls inevitably stirs the surface waters with political partisanship among otherwise well-intentioned leaders.

Individual Worth

The inherent worth of one individual is another spiritual assumption with powerful implications for public policy. It is not a universal precept for there are centuries-old traditions held by multitudes on earth who do not share this value of one person's welfare. At no other time in the history of nations, civilizations, empires, or tribal governance has there been such a reverence for the value of one solitary individual as there is in the Western world. Our laws and our welfare policies (however successful) all reflect our absolute reverence for the value of one solitary individual. It is difficult to explain this reverence for one person's worth and the consequent rights it implies apart from the biblical concept of the vicarious nature of Isaiah's suffering servant or of Christ's death for the sins of one solitary, sinful human. This value of the individual, which is codified in a hundred places in our policies, does not have a long history. Nor is it necessarily rational. In fact, it flies in the face of much of nature which tends to reward the self-serving survivor. To so value the individual is not the result of scientific logic, but a derivative of faith. It is captured in a genre of specific policies which reflects clearly spiritual assumptions.

Equality

Equality under the law and the preference for equality of opportunity which is so deeply embedded in the public policies of the United States—and by influence and imitation in a growing number of other nations—also reflects a spiritual assumption. Most of human history has been a record of how the strong and fortunate have constructed institutions and policies and cultures to favor some over others. Jesus was criticized constantly for his ministry not only to the powerful and rich, but to those thrown on the garbage heap of society. Each was precious because each was his brother or sister, a child of God. Today, this assumption of equal treatment, opportunity, and worth is embedded in numerous policy initiatives. But when it was stated crisply by the Apostle Paul, it was an absolutely radical idea: "In Christ Jesus, you are all sons of God, through faith. . . . There is neither Jew nor Greek, there is neither slave nor free, there is neither male nor female; for you are all one in Christ Jesus."[2]

Public Policy and Secular Humanism

The irony of the century we have just closed is that what we expected to be the triumph of our civilization has, in fact, been the disintegration of our culture. For many, the celebrated democratic freedom of liberal society has ended, in reality, in servitude to popular illusions which are cynical toward religious faith. Excessive centralization of public policy has, in fact, not only destroyed community, but failed its high objectives and undermined the moral glue of our civilization which, in times past, was found in faith. T. S. Eliot and others have predicted that the success of secular humanists in capturing so many of the policies which have gained the support of our institutions of government will lead us again into another Dark Age. There is no evidence in history that progress toward civility is either inevitable or permanent.

Another effort which has failed has been the search for some form of "civil religion." Russell Kirk, in one of his lectures at the Heritage Foundation toward the close of his life, noted that

> Some well-meaning folk talk of a "civil religion," a kind of cult of patriotism, founded upon a myth of national virtue and upon veneration of certain historic documents, together with a utilitarian morality. But such experiments of a secular character never have functioned satisfactorily. And it scarcely is necessary for me to point out the perils of such an artificial creed, bound up with nationalism. The example of the ideology of the National Socialist Party in Germany, half a century ago, may suffice. Worship of the state, or of the national commonwealth, is no healthy substitute for communion with transcendent love and wisdom.[3]

Signs of Hope

But for the faithful, moments of crisis present opportunities for courage, for hope, and for rebirth. Christopher Dawson, in his book, *Religion and Culture*, wrote that

> the recovery of moral control and the return to spiritual order have become the indispensable conditions of human survival. But they can be achieved only by a profound change in the spirit of modern civilization. This does not mean a new religion or a new culture, but a movement of spiritual reintegration which would restore that vital relation between religion and culture which has existed at every age and on every level of human development.[4]

We have tried moral relativism and neutrality as well as idolatrous scientism. We have tried vast centralized and costly federal programs which provided full employment to administrators but devastation to the family and to our educational system. But in the darkness that these efforts have thrown over us, there remain rays of hope. There is a growing body of evidence that a reenergized faith and a return to nongovernmental organizations in fact is offering new hope for successful public policy based on new paradigms which are not really new, but a rediscovery of the old.

Nor does this sweeping spirit of reform require massive legislation or a vast army of government agents. Again, Russell Kirk has observed that "American Civilization of our era is rooted, strange though the fact may seem to us, in tiny knots of worshippers in Palestine, Greece, and Italy, thousands of years ago. The enormous material achievements of our civilization have resulted, if remotely, from the spiritual insights of prophets and seers."[5]

I recently visited the humble ruins of the synagogue in Capernaum and strolled the shore where Jesus most assuredly called his early disciples to become fishers of men. I crossed over the Syrian Sea at Galilee in a boat similar to one Jesus must have used and was moved again by the power of spiritual ideas turned loose in this obscure region to alter the lives of multitudes on every continent. In fact, as Russell Kirk observed, even today, our search is for the prophets for our age—some remnant on which to build a new sense of hope.

The research of John DiIulio and others, detailed in subsequent chapters, is strongly suggesting that one of the brightest prospects on our horizon is in the area of faith-based social programs. Most of the preliminary evidence, according to DiIulio, is encouraging, including studies showing that churched young black urban males have lower rates of crime, drugs, and joblessness than unchurched youth. Faith-based programs in prisons also demonstrate measurable rehabilitative results.

The Welfare Reform Act of 1996 encourages states to engage faith-based organizations as providers of welfare, job search programs, maternity homes for expectant unmarried minors, drug treatment programs, and much more. Under what is called the charitable choice provision, religious providers may, under clearly defined circumstances, accept government funds without renouncing their religious character.

Advances in public policy which will immediately impact our largest problems must include cooperation among diverse institutions. The answer most likely must be found not in one sector, but in a relationship among many sectors that is mutually supportive and understanding. Faith, after all, is not one element among many—not a way of dealing with certain things—but a certain way of dealing with everything.

It is tempting to hope for yet another "Great Awakening," a revival of faith in reaction to the corruptions of contemporary society. Certainly, I do not believe that God is through with the human race. Nor do I believe this nation is through with its mission in his larger plan. Liberty and human dignity advance in bursts of energy rather than in a predictable pattern. Like lightning, liberty fractures the foul tempest of history to choose its own unstructured path and deliver its unique message. It then passes on, like a charged cloud, moving across the landscape of history, hoarding moral energy for its next strike on its own conductive high ground. It chooses its unexpected target in the desert—its church, its clan, its university, its codes of Hammurabi and Confucius, its Magna Carta and Declaration of Independence, its sacred stones of Islam and Sinai, its Kilimanjaro and Uluru, its Golgotha, its cast-out remnant of homeless gypsies— to pierce the darkness. Then, in the fullness of time, liberty selects its one-of-a-kind—its woman or man, its child in a manger—and discharges energy to earth, God into flesh.

All the while, as this epoch of God is played out, the empire builders and institution keepers, the policy codifiers and entombers of energy, squander memorials to cadavers on life support systems: the apostate church, the tenured university turning in upon itself, the government once energized by the freedom fighters it now seeks to imprison or destroy. These encrusted institutions will waste tears on places once struck by history passing by, will miss the dance of God across the sky to the next excommunicated one, and use up a lifetime waiting for lightning to strike twice. Meanwhile, the spiritual forces underlying public policies will germinate, await their *kairos*, their fullness of time, and work God's will. The only question is to what extent we as individuals, and the United States of America as a nation, will be willing instruments of his transcendent purpose.

Notes

1. Richard Weaver, *Ideas Have Consequences* (Chicago: University of Chicago Press, 1948).

2. Gal. 3:26-28 (RSV).

3. Russell Kirk, "Civilization Without Religion?" *Heritage Lecture* 404 (Washington, D.C., 21 August 1992).

4. Christopher Dawson, *Religion and Culture*, second ed. (London: Sheed and Ward, 1949), 218.

5. Kirk, *Heritage Lecture.*

Part I

The Founding:
Faith of Our Fathers

Chapter 2

The Continuing Revolution: What We Can Learn from the Founding Fathers

Jack Scott

Many people ask me how I have been affected by becoming a member of the state legislature of California. Frankly, this is a new experience for me. I am a citizen legislator, not a career politician. In fact, the *Reader's Digest* not long ago had sketches of citizen legislators, and I was honored to be one of those mentioned.

Previously, I spent thirty-six years in higher education. During that time I did not picture myself in politics. But when I was asked to run for public office, I finally decided I could make an impact, particularly in the field of education. I ran and was fortunate enough to win. Now, when people ask me what it is like, I'm reminded of a story in the life of Mark Twain. Twain as a young man had left his home in Missouri and had gone to Carson City, Nevada. After being there for several months, he wrote back to one of his friends: "Carson City, Nevada is really some place. Liquor flows very freely here. A loose woman is on almost every corner and gambling is going on twenty-four hours a day. This place is no place for a good Presbyterian—therefore, I no longer am one."[1]

I hope politics has not corrupted me in the same way. Actually, I have enjoyed my life in Sacramento and, in the era of term limits, it suits me fine. I hope to make a contribution to the state and then move on.

I was pleased when I was asked to discuss the Founding Fathers at this Faith and Public Policy conference. I have a particular interest in this subject since my Ph.D. is in American history and my doctoral dissertation was written about one of the signers of the Declaration of Independence, John Witherspoon. John Witherspoon was the only clergyman to sign the Declaration of Independence. He was the president of the College of New Jersey, which later became Princeton University.

9

I have been in college administration since completing my Ph.D., so I have not kept up with the scholarship of the Founding Fathers as much as I would like. However, I still have a keen interest, not only in public policy, but particularly in religion in American life.

There is no question that religion profoundly affected public policy from the earliest days of our nation. It was one of the primary impulses behind the colonization of North America. This is true whether one is considering the missions in California or the eastern colonization of the shores of the United States. The Pilgrims came in 1620 to seek a religious haven. They had earlier immigrated to Holland and then came to this continent. The founder and governor of the Massachusetts Bay Colony established in 1630 was John Winthrop. I quote from an essay he wrote as he and his fellow colonists sailed to America:

> [t]hat men shall say of succeeding plantations [he is speaking of settlements] the Lord make it like that of New England for we shall be as a City upon a Hill. The eyes of all people are upon us, so that if we shall deal falsely with our God in this work we have undertaken and so cause Him to withdraw His present help from us, we shall be made a story and by-word through the world."[2]

You can sense their mission: They were in covenant with God and they were a chosen people. This sense of chosenness has continued throughout American history. You can read it in the Manifest Destiny of the nineteenth century as America came to believe it was a chosen people moving out across the continent to the Pacific Ocean. And it is clear in the words of Woodrow Wilson when the United States entered World War I when he said our intent was "to make the world safe for democracy." The imagery that comes from the Old Testament of "a chosen people" is an integral trait in American life.

However, I must avoid overstating this. Certainly not everyone who immigrated to America in the colonial days came for religious reasons. There were also economic motivations. One looks at the rich agricultural land of the South filled with the crops of tobacco, rice, and indigo which eventually led, unfortunately, to African slavery in the colonies. By the time of the American Revolution, one out of every five colonists was an African slave.

As an example of the motivation of trade and commerce, I think of John Hancock, the great shipping magnate. He and others left Europe because they were either in great debt or they wanted to escape imprisonment. It was an interesting set of circumstances that they left behind.

But religion in colonial American life was still central. I would call it the most significant thread in the tapestry of colonial life. Eight out of nine colonial colleges were founded for religious reasons, beginning with Harvard in 1636. In fact, the only one of the nine not founded for religious purposes was the University of Pennsylvania, which was established by Benjamin Franklin. The convergence of religion and education is a powerful demonstration of the impact of religious conviction upon colonial life.

Now we turn beyond the colonial period to the beginning of our country in the late eighteenth century. One can look at two central documents that were important as our foundation documents: The Declaration of Independence and the Constitution both have strong religious assumptions. The Declaration of Independence embraced the concept of natural law. Natural law held that a government was formed as a result of people freely coming together and forming a community. And natural law suggested that even without revelation (e.g., the Bible), individuals had a natural sense of morality that had been given to them by God, including the belief that they had certain rights. Note the concept of natural law in these words of the Declaration of Independence: "to assume . . . the separate and equal station to which the laws of nature and of nature's God entitle them. . . . Governments are instituted among men, deriving their just powers from the consent of the governed." And there is the famous phrase where Jefferson proclaims "that they are endowed by their Creator with certain inalienable rights; that among these are life, liberty, and the pursuit of happiness." These are God-given rights. They affirmed that God was involved in the founding of the nation, the God in whose providence these men believed. To illustrate further, note the concluding words of the Declaration of Independence: "And for the support of this declaration, with a firm reliance on the protection of Divine Providence, we mutually pledge to each other our lives, our fortunes, and our sacred honor."[3]

What I am underscoring is the way in which religion permeated the formation of the Declaration of Independence. In fact, the very war that the colonists waged against England had to be theologically justified. It is not an easy thing for people to decide to take up arms. After all, there is the possibility not only of their own death, but of their killing others. Thus, the American colonies took up arms with some reluctance. But in order to do it and to feel right about it, they had to feel that God could justify armed rebellion under certain circumstances.

The colonists had the historical memory of the seventeenth-century rebellion in England and the Puritan revolution. In this revolution, the English overthrew the king and actually beheaded Charles I, and this ushered in the rule of Oliver Cromwell when they had no king. Later, the monarchy was restored in 1660, but kings never again had the kind of power they had possessed before that time. This power was offset by the Parliament.

So are there circumstances which justify Christians taking up arms? The subject of my dissertation, John Witherspoon, lectured to his college seniors even before the time of the Revolution about the right of rebellion. As a Presbyterian minister, he said that under certain circumstances it was justified. Notice his line of reasoning: [i]f the supreme power wherever lodged come to be exercised in a manifestly tyrannical manner, the subjects may certainly if in their power resist and overthrow it. . . . If it be asked who must judge when the government may be resisted, I answer the subjects in general, everyone for himself. . . . [i]t is not till a whole people rise, that the resistance has any effect."[4] In a practical matter he was affirming that you cannot have a rebellion if only a few of you engage in it. But if the powers that be are excessively tyrannical, then there comes a time when there is sufficient rationale for taking up arms. "In experience there are many instances of rulers becoming tyrants, but comparatively, very few of causeless and premature rebellions."[5]

Notice closely what he is saying. He is simply making the point that it is unlikely that there will be many rebellions that have insufficient cause. Therefore, if the tyranny is great enough, then people are justified in taking up arms.

That is, of course, exactly what the Declaration of Independence contends: that when any form of government becomes destructive of these ends, it is the right of the people to alter or abolish it and institute a new government. Thus, they felt justified in their armed rebellion.

If you remember your American history, you know that the Declaration was signed on July 4, 1776. But the armed conflict actually began in April of 1775. There was still the hope that the colonists could rebel and the king would grant them the freedoms that they wanted and that they still would be his subjects. It was only after the winter of 1775-76 and the failed Olive Branch Petition that the colonists gave up on reaching settlement with the home country. Therefore, they were willing to declare their independence.

Contemporary Implications

There are many modern implications which we could discuss. One tenet that was preeminent in America and which caused it to become a beacon to the entire world was the matter of religious freedom. One would have to rewrite American history, however, if one suggested that all those people who first settled here in the seventeenth century believed in religious freedom. For instance, many of the Puritans clearly did not. The Puritans drove Roger Williams out of Massachusetts and into Rhode Island because he was an advocate of religious freedom. And Quakers were actually hanged for their heretical views.

But as time went on, there were many advocates of religious freedom—one striking example is William Penn, the great Quaker who founded the Pennsylvania colony. And even the Calverts of Maryland, who were of Catholic background, became advocates for religious freedom. Slowly the principle of religious freedom permeated the United States, not only for philosophical reasons, but for practical reasons as well. When you have a country that is as pluralistic as the colonies were, when you have Baptists, Methodists, Presbyterians, Puritans, and others, there comes a time when you must conclude that it would be difficult to enforce uniformity. Thus, religious freedom is written into the First Amendment of the Constitution: "Congress shall make no law respecting an establishment of religion, or prohibiting the free exercise thereof."

There are many implications of that principle. I think of the 1940 court case involving the Jehovah's Witness children in school who would not salute the flag. According to their religious views, such a pledge was considering the flag as an idol. There may be many of us who would find their view distasteful, but there is no doubt that this was an issue of religious freedom. And when it finally reached the Supreme Court, the conclusion was that if it is against their religious beliefs to do so, they cannot be forced to pledge allegiance to the flag.[6] This is a particularly valuable lesson for us today because of the increasing pluralism of this nation. And, we have to go beyond the pluralism of Christian groups of the early days of the United States, for in America today we find more and more non-Christian groups. In Chicago, for instance, there are now fifteen mosques. You can drive down nearby Malibu Canyon Road in Los Angeles County and see a Hindu temple. So the principle of religious freedom still serves as a model for twentieth-century America.

Another principle from early America is the separation of church and state. There is a difference here between religious freedom and the separation of church and state. To quote again from the First Amendment: "Congress shall make no law respecting an establishment of religion."[7] We may take that for granted, but in Europe at that time it was believed that the state should support the church and that a uniformity of religious belief helped produce uniformity in civil society. There were many European nations that just could not envision the possibility of a variety of religious beliefs and still have the country unified. So it was rather natural that countries like France and Spain were Catholic, while England was led by the Church of England and the Scandinavian countries were Lutheran.

Even the states of Connecticut and Massachusetts did not completely abolish the establishment of religion until the nineteenth century. There was a very heated controversy at the beginning of our nation about this issue. Patrick Henry felt very strongly that churches should be supported by the state. But James Madison took the other side in a famous Virginia debate. Madison stated:

> Because the establishment proposed by the Bill [i.e., Patrick Henry's bill] is not requisite for the support of the Christian Religion, to say that it is, is a contradiction to the Christian Religion itself. For every page of it disavows a dependence upon the powers of this world. It is a contradiction of fact, for it is known that this Religion [i.e., Christianity] both existed and flourished, not only without the support of human laws, but in spite of every opposition from them.[8]

That debate occurred in 1786 and by 1787 it was clear that the sentiment in the Constitutional Convention was in favor of the separation of church and state. It proved to have great value for the power of religion in our country to avoid an entanglement with the state. Furthermore, it encouraged great vitality of religious bodies because they became dependent on the voluntary contributions of their membership rather than on the state itself. In fact, Alexis de Tocqueville, that famous French observer who came to America in 1829-1830 and who wrote the book, *Democracy in America*, said, "All thought the main reason for the quiet sway of religion over the country was the complete separation of church and state. I have no hesitation in stating that throughout my stay in America I met nobody, lay or cleric, who did not agree with that."[9]

While this is only a small look at the Founding Fathers, let me add just one caveat here. I think that there are some things we ought to avoid when we think of the Founding Fathers. We should not, for instance, hold them to a standard of perfection. After all, many were slaveholders. But they were a remarkable group of principled men, I would even say geniuses, who came together at a fortuitous time in history. Remember that at its beginning, America had a population of fewer than five million people. Yet when we observe the remarkable leaders such as George Washington, Thomas Jefferson, John Adams, James Madison, Alexander Hamilton, and Benjamin Franklin, we are immediately struck by how wonderful—shall we say providential—that such leaders should have come together at the beginning of a nation. To be sure, they made some mistakes. Nor did they view the Constitution as a sacred document. In fact, they left room for amendment; remember when it was first passed, the Constitution did not have the Bill of Rights. But they had the Bill of Rights in mind and these were quickly added. And since that time, there have been sixteen further amendments added to the Constitution.

Also, I must point out that it is a mistake to label all these men as religious conservatives. They were religious. Of this, there is no question. But it is also clear that some were Deists, like Washington, Jefferson, and Franklin. By Deists I mean they had the belief that God started the world and that God would then simply oversee the world. But they did not believe in an interventionist God. Listen to the words of Franklin in his famous autobiography. He was originally a Presbyterian but found some of the views of the Presbyterian Church difficult to accept. So he wrote,

> I early absented myself from the Public Assemblies of the Sect, Sunday being my Studying-Day, I never was without some religious Principles. I never doubted, for instance, the Existance of the Deity, that he made the World and governed by his Providence; that the most acceptable Service of God was the doing of Good to Man; that our Souls are immortal; and that all Crime will be punished, and Virtue rewarded, either here or hereafter.[10]

What we have in the Constitution is an organic document. It is the creed and the foundation of our country—not a sacred document, but a document that must constantly be reinterpreted. After all, the law of the land is not only the Constitution, but the subsequent interpretation of the Supreme Court. The federal constitution is a summation of general principles. It is the work of the Supreme Court to translate these general principles into concrete constitutional demands.

In fact, sometimes the Supreme Court has differed from decade to decade. *Plessy v. Ferguson,* in 1896, ruled that there could be separate but equal education for different races. But in 1954, in *Brown v. Topeka*, the Court reversed that.

What are the implications for today? First, we can be justly proud as Americans of a great and wonderful heritage. In fact, no nation other than England has existed for two-hundred years as the United States has without a change of government. Think of the frequent turnover and change in countries like France, Italy, or Germany. Yet we have been a nation, founded with the Constitution in 1787, which has celebrated its bicentennial. And although we have had our ups and downs, even torn at one time by civil war, we have continued.

Many of today's policies reflect the Founding Father's principles. I believe that one of the central tenets of our nation is that great declaration, "All men are created equal."[11] This is really a religious principle. You can find it in the lines of Paul when he says that in Jesus Christ there is neither Greek nor Jew, bond nor free, male nor female. And when you stop to think about it, in many ways the history of the United States is a continuous effort to attain that vision. Remember that at the start, the vote was only held by propertied white males. Slowly impediments to the right to vote were removed. By the time of Andrew Jackson, a greater democracy was achieved as more and more males were given the right of vote. And then after the Civil War the vote was given to African Americans after the slaves had been freed. In the twentieth century the right to vote was extended to women.

Even in recent times, certain movements grew out of this principle of equality, notably the civil rights movement. Martin Luther King, Jr., often played a significant role in extending freedom, basing it on religious principles. His imagery compared African Americans to those who were in Egyptian slavery. He said that morally we had given a "bad check to the Negro people." Later this principle was extended to those who suffered disabilities. And women have often stated that the belief in gender equality is a moral principle, even a religious principle.

We have also cited the principles of democracy in going to war. We have never based conflict on the principle that we are a powerful nation and we can simply take what we want. We have had to ask whether or not this is the right thing to do. One of America's most religious presidents was Abraham Lincoln. He was religious in the best sense of the word. He was not self-righteous; he questioned what he was doing, realizing that he could be wrong. Note the way in which religion informed what he had to say in the Second Inaugural Address as the Civil War was coming to a close:

Fondly do we hope—fervently do we pray—that this mighty scourge of war may speedily pass away. Yet, if God wills that it continue, until all the wealth piled by the bondsman's two hundred and fifty years of unrequiting toil shall be sunk, and until every drop of blood drawn with the lash be paid by another drawn with the sword, as was said three thousand years ago, so still it must be said "the judgments of the Lord are true and righteous altogether." With malice toward none; with charity for all; with firmness in the right, as God gives us to see the right, let us strive on to finish the work we are in; to bind up the nation's wounds; to care for him who shall have borne the battle, and for his widow, and his orphan—to do all which may achieve and cherish a just, and a lasting peace, among ourselves, and with all nations.[12]

So religion was important in the Civil War. And religion is important to the issues we face today. Moral values impact what we do in terms of public policy—whether we are discussing the issue of welfare, or the issue of abortion, or the issue of the regulation of guns. All these things have moral concerns behind them.

Jack Scott

None of these issues is simplistic. I remember some years ago seeing a bumper sticker which read, "The Bible says it, I believe it, that settles it." Well, it's not quite that easy. I do not think most of us believe that the dietary laws of Leviticus are as binding as the Sermon on the Mount. We have to interpret the Bible, as we must employ interpretation when working with the Constitution. There is a difference between separating church from state on the one hand and divorcing religion totally from public policy on the other.

Frankly, this means that my religious views impact legislation. As a legislator, they impact the way that I initiate policy and the way that I vote. Let me illustrate this. Recently, on the floor of the Assembly I introduced a bill on adoption. This bill made adoption easier, with less bureaucratic red tape for those who are foster parents to adopt the children under their care. What motivated me to introduce such a bill? First, I saw a problem. But secondly, it is my conviction that children are best cared for in the home. The statistics indicate that only one out of eight foster children remain in the same foster home for the entire period of their childhood. But ninety-nine out of one hundred who are adopted remain in the same home. What can we do to encourage that? It was the love of children that led me to that legislation. That is a simple demonstration that moral values help us in matters of voting and introducing legislation.

As another example, we begin every day in the state assembly with a prayer. I am hopeful that through that prayer we have greater wisdom. It does not always triumph, but at least we can hope for that. In fact, G. K. Chesterton one time referred to the United States as a "nation with the soul of a church."[13]

But the soul of a church is different from a theocracy. I am always frightened by a theocracy. A theocracy is when one religious group takes control and fastens its views on the rest of the nation. We have seen this phenomenon among right-wing fundamentalist Islamic people. In Iran, Khomeini got control and suddenly many other religions were persecuted and people's lives were placed in oppressive, binding circumstances. The zealotry of fundamentalism, whether it be ultra-orthodox Judaism in Israel or people in our own country who believe that they have the truth cornered, that they have discovered the final answer, should frighten us all. Although the Bible suggests that there is absolute truth, it does not suggest that any human being has grasped it completely.

This is why a certain humility is appropriate. As Paul would say, we know "in part" and we prophesy "in part." He would describe our present state as seeing through a glass darkly. As I look back on my own personal life over the past thirty years, I have changed some of my beliefs. Perhaps if I had possessed absolute power in my youth of thirty years ago, I would now regret enforcing those beliefs on others. And that is why we were blessed by the Founding Fathers and their core belief in religious freedom. People who can exercise religious freedom have the right to view and to worship their Creator as they believe they should. Furthermore, the state and the church have to avoid entanglements. This separation brings vitality to the church and it also keeps the state from becoming an instrument of any one particular religious view.

In conclusion, the Founding Fathers genuinely created a revolution, a revolution that not only impacted America but has been felt throughout the world. The words of the Declaration of Independence are often quoted on the continents of Africa, Europe, Asia, and all over the world. So we are constantly enriched by the thoughts of our Founding Fathers, and we can be very proud as Americans to have this wonderful heritage.

Notes

1. Mark Twain (Samuel Clemens), *Roughing It* (Hartford, Conn.: American Publishing Co., 1891), 302-4.

2. John Winthrop, "A Modell of Christian Charity" (1630), in *The Founding of Massachusetts: Historians and the Sources*, ed. Edmund S. Morgan (Indianapolis: Bobbs-Merrill Company, 1964), 203.

3. Declaration of Independence.

4. John Witherspoon, *The Selected Writings of John Witherspoon*, ed. Thomas Miller (Carbondale, Ill.: Southern Illinois University Press, 1990), 204.

5. Miller, *Selected Writings of Witherspoon*.

6. *Minersville School District v. Board of Education*, 310 U.S. 586 (1940).

7. United States Constitution, First Amendment.

8. James Madison, "Memorial and Remonstrance Against Religious Assessments" (1785), in *The Complete Madison: His Basic Writings*, ed. Saul K. Padover (New York: Harper & Bros., 1953; New York: Kraus Reprint Co., 1971), 302.

9. Alexis de Tocqueville, *Democracy in America*, trans. George Lawrence, ed. J. P. Mayer (New York: Harper Collins Perennial Classics, 2000), 295.

10. *The Autobiography of Benjamin Franklin*, second ed., ed. Leonard W. Labaree, Ralph L. Ketcham, Helen C. Boatfield, and Helene H. Fineman (New Haven, Conn.: Yale University Press, 1967), 145-46.

11. Declaration of Independence.

12. Abraham Lincoln, "Second Inaugural Address," in *The Collected Works of Abraham Lincoln*, Vol. 8 (New Brunswick, N.J.: Rutgers University Press, 1953), 333.

13. G. K. Chesterton, *What I Saw in America* (New York: Dodd, Mead, and Co., 1922), 11-20.

Chapter 3

God's Country:
Taking the Declaration Seriously

Michael Novak

On the first Sunday of Advent, the church bells of Rome began pealing, clanging, tolling the opening of the third millennium, marking thus the birth of a Jewish infant born in poverty. The impact of that helpless child upon the world has no parallel in history.

Through him knowledge of the Creator who knows and attends to individual nations and individual persons was spread to the Gentiles: a vision of a benign Governor of the universe, a most gracious Providence, the undeceivable Judge of the consciences of all, the Source of Nature's Laws, the Guarantor through sacred oaths of the truthfulness of systems of justice. Through him the Law of Moses became, as Blackstone put it, the font and spring of constitutional government.[1]

This God endowed in every woman and every man inalienable rights. The "God Who gave us life," Jefferson wrote, "gave us liberty at the same time."[2]

Five thousand years of belief in such a God, Alfred North Whitehead observed, made possible the rise of modern science.[3] The call to imitate the Creator imparted to discovery, invention, and creativity a profound and palpable joy. David Landes, in *The Wealth and Poverty of Nations*, says that the Jewish-Christian "joy of discovery" was as responsible as any other factor for the economic breakthroughs of the West.[4]

And yet we come to the new millennium with a heavy question: Does the century about to begin mark our last? Is America a meteor that has blazed across the heavens, now exhausted? Or, rather, is our present moral fog a transient time of trial, those hours cold and dark before the ramparts' new gleaming? Are we nearing our end or at a new beginning?

19

Looking Back One Hundred Years

Just a century ago 50 percent of the seventy-five million people of the United States lived in rural areas. Most people had no plumbing, electricity, or any transport except the horse. Ordinary people endured cold, heat, darkness, stench, crowding, spoilage. On the other hand, 80 percent of households were headed by a married couple, and the federal government spent about 2 percent of the gross national product.[5]

In the one hundred years since then, the United States has been much tested: from the harsh and bitter shock of Verdun; from the lows of the Depression, through the agonies of Omaha Beach; from tail-fins, Ike, and Elvis to flower children and the march on the Pentagon; from the biting cold of the Korean Peninsula to the steaming heat of Quang Ngai; from the "Letter from a Birmingham Jail" to the Chairman of the Joint Chiefs Colin Powell; from McCarthyism to the collapse of the myth of socialist inevitability, when the Berlin Wall came down; from the Reagan tax cuts to the greatest extended prosperity in American history. Technologies we never heard of thirty years ago characterize our lives today: word processors, faxes, cell phones, e-mail, biogenetics.

Along this short road of one hundred years, we have become powerful and rich. And what about our nation's soul? Five subterranean earthquakes have altered the ecology of souls.

- Our great Protestant elite lost its self-confidence in its religious convictions following World War II. The old Yankee elite of Boston, Philadelphia, and New York no longer sets the nation's moral tone.
- Remember the erudite, eloquent letters written by soldiers of the Civil War, educated in one-room schoolhouses and by the Bible? Then watch MTV. Our moral ethos has fallen into the hands of "popular culture."
- Throughout the last century, Europe looked up to America as a model for the world. In this century, our intellectual class has looked up to Europe as the model for America—social democracy, the welfare state, Sweden.
- Beginning in 1947, in the guise of becoming "neutral," our courts and law schools became hostile to religion in the public square.

- Confined by the courts to private quarters, religious people who act in public spaces are rebuked with ridicule and penalties in university employment and in the law.

Jolted by these five institutional upheavals, in a brief fifty years the great well of religious and moral self-awareness of the American public has been emptied of its living water.

Few today can understand the American proposition in the way our forebears understood it. Words central to the American creed, such as truth ("we hold these truths"), liberty ("conceived in liberty"), law ("liberty under law"), and judge ("appealing to the Supreme Judge of the World for the rectitude of our intentions") once formed a great and glorious mosaic across the apse of the republic. That mosaic has fallen to the dust, disassembled into tiny pieces. Fewer every year remember how it used to look.

we have separated ourselves from what the country was based on

The Present Crisis

As a disturbing consequence, nonreligious people are growing more hostile to the remaining Jewish and Christian impulses they detect in public life. Some portray religious people as outside "the American way," extremists whose aim is to impose "theocracy."

An opposite consequence is that serious religious people are becoming alienated from the American polity. This U.S.A. (they say) is not the partner with whom our forebears made a covenant. *This* is not an ethos we admire. We know and we admire Philadelphia, 1787, but that culture lives no more.

Other citizens want not to be judged by anyone. They abhor "judgmentalism." The ancient biblical maxim, "Judge not, lest ye be judged," implied that God's standards are high. The modern maxim forbids standards altogether (they are harmful to self-esteem).

Thus has the ancient Jewish, Christian (and modern) virtue of tolerance been undone. Tolerance used to mean that people of strong convictions would willingly bear the burden of putting up peacefully with people they regarded as plainly in error. Now it means that people of weak convictions facilely agree that others are also right, and anyway the truth of things doesn't make much difference, as long as everyone is "nice." I don't know if "judgmentaphobic" is a word, but it ought to be. This republic crawls with judgmentaphobes. Where conscience used to raise an eyebrow at our slips and falls, sunny non-judgmentalism winks and slaps us on the back.

In the absence of judgment, however, freedom cannot thrive. If nothing matters, freedom is pointless. If one choice is as good as another, choice is merely preference. A glandular reflex would do as well. Without standards, no one is free, but only a slave of impulses coming from who knows where. This is sometimes dignified as the scientific view of man.

To the contrary, the whole point of liberty is this: Every choice makes a difference, for the fate of every soul and for the fate of the republic.

Nature highlights liberty; it is unique to human beings. The God of Abraham, Isaac, and Jacob, says the Bible, values liberty so mightily that he created this vast expanding cosmos to show it off. So that somewhere in it, in at least one place, there would be creatures free to recognize their Creator's friendship and freely walk with him.

The Creator called humans to build a city on a hill (a "shining city on a hill," as Ronald Reagan taught us to amend it).

This Creator called humans to learn from history how to build, eventually, a republic of liberty and justice for all: a city, at last, worthy of such creatures as he had fashioned. They would have to do this by trial and error.

Fittingly, when the time was ripe, after the passage of thousands of years, in a city named for the second Great Commandment, "Thou shalt love thy neighbor as thyself"—in Philadelphia—the independence of such a republic was proclaimed, invoking his just judgment and asking his protection. Will that protection last forever?

All history is proof of a law of moral entropy. Civilizations, given time, end badly. Surrounded in Washington by monuments that echo Greece and Rome, we are reminded daily of the fall of great republics and democracies. What hope have we that our nation will end differently?

There are lessons in this nation's covenant with God, of which the Declaration of Independence is the primary jewel.

The Covenant

During the first days of September 1774, from every region, members of the First Continental Congress were riding dustily toward Philadelphia, where they hoped to remind King George III of the rights due them as Englishmen. As these delegates were gathering, news arrived that Charlestown had been raked by cannonshot, and red-coated landing parties had surged through its streets.

The gathering delegates proposed a motion for public prayer, that all might gain in sobriety and wisdom. Mr. Jay of New York and Mr. Rutledge of South Carolina spoke against this motion because Americans are so divided in religious sentiments, some Episcopalians, some Quakers, some Anabaptists, some Presbyterians, and some Congregationalists, that all could not join in the same act of worship. Sam Adams arose to say he was no bigot and could hear a prayer from any gentleman of piety and virtue, who was at the same time a friend to his country. Mr. Adams was a stranger in Philadelphia, but had heard that a certain Rev. Duché had earned that character, and moved that the same be asked to read prayers to Congress on the morrow. The motion carried.

Thus it happened that on September 7, 1774, the first official prayer before the Continental Congress was pronounced by a white-haired Episcopal clergyman dressed in his pontificals, who read aloud from the Book of Common Prayer the thirty-fifth Psalm: "Plead my cause, O Lord, with them that strive with me, fight against them that fight against me. Take hold of buckler and shield, and rise up for my help. . . . Say to my soul, 'I am your salvation.' Let those be ashamed and dishonored who seek my life; let those be turned back and humiliated who devise evil against me."

Before him knelt Washington, Henry, Randolph, Rutledge, Lee, and Jay, and by their side, heads bowed, the Puritan patriots, who could imagine at that moment their homes being bombarded and overrun. Over these bowed heads the Reverend Duché uttered what all testified was an eloquent prayer, "for America, for Congress, for the Province of Massachusetts Bay, and especially for the town of Boston." The emotion in the room was palpable, and John Adams wrote to Abigail that he "had never heard a better prayer, or one so well pronounced. I never saw a greater effect upon an audience. It seemed as if heaven had ordained that Psalm to be read on that morning. . . . It was enough to melt a heart of stone. I saw tears gush into the eyes of the old, grave pacific Quakers of Philadelphia. . . . I must beg you to read that Psalm."[6]

In this fashion, right at its beginning, this nation formed a covenant with God, which it repeated in the Declaration ("with a firm Reliance on the Protection of Divine Providence") and in many later acts of Congress regarding Days of Fasting (for repentance) or Thanksgiving.[7] Let me quote from the Day of Fasting, December 11, 1776: "Resolved, That it be recommended to all the United States, as soon as possible, to appoint a day of solemn fasting and humiliation; to implore of Almighty God the forgiveness of the many sins prevailing among all ranks, and to beg the countenance and assistance of his Providence in the prosecution of the present just and necessary war."[8]

Years later, in *The Federalist* No. 38, Publius marveled at the unanimity improbably achieved among fragmented delegates from free states and slave, from small states and large, from rich states and poor: "It is impossible for the man of pious reflection not to perceive in it a finger of the Almighty hand which has been so frequently and signally extended to our relief in the critical stages of the revolution." Three times *The Federalist* notes the blessings of Providence upon this country.[9]

This has been our covenant with God. God wills free peoples to build communities in cities that gleam upon the hills, cities of virtue, and probity, and honor. God knows we are only fallen human beings, clay, poor materials for so grand a task. No matter. He calls on us.

Among the nations, no people has embraced this covenant so gladly as Americans. Their brightest jewel was the Declaration.

The Declaration

On July 2, 1776, the Continental Congress voted, and on July 4 proclaimed the Declaration of Independence of the United States. In that document, Thomas Jefferson twice referred to God in biblical terms, and before assenting to it, the Congress added two more references.[10]

The fifty-six signers were, mostly, Christians; they represented a mostly Christian people; and it was from Christian traditions that they had learned these names. But the names of God they chose were entirely of Jewish provenance. Of names specific to the Christian faith the signers were (wisely) silent, since it lies not in the competence of government to adjudicate theological differences beyond those essential for the common good.

Recall the four names that these Americans gave to God: *Lawgiver* (as in "Laws of Nature and Nature's God"); *Creator* ("endowed by their Creator with certain inalienable rights"); *Judge* ("appealing to the Supreme Judge of the World for the Rectitude of our Intentions"); and *Providence* ("with a firm Reliance on the Protection of divine Providence").

Michael Novak

One of these names for God ("Lawgiver") could be considered Greek or Roman. But Richard Hooker showed that long tradition had put "Lawgiver," too, in a biblical context.[11] The other three names (Creator, Judge, Providence) derive from Judaism and came to America via Protestant Christianity.

That is not all. Implicit throughout the Declaration are four biblical *paradigms*: ways of imagining reality. First, this world had a *beginning*, was not an eternal cycle. Second, it was *created*, was not an accident. Third, on the entire cosmos was bestowed an intelligent and gracious purpose, a Providence. Fourth, this *purpose* of creation was to place human liberty in a kind of holy light, as captured in the hymn "America":

> Our fathers' God! To Thee,
> Author of liberty,
> To Thee we sing.
> Long may our land be bright
> With *freedom's* holy light;
> Protect us by Thy might,
> Great God our king.[12]

These four conceptions are neither Greek nor Roman notions. They are biblical. They arose from Judaism. Jerusalem, not Athens, is their birthplace. They gave our forebears an almost eerie confidence.

The God of liberty is not, and cannot be, a remote watchmaker God. Examine closely the God of the framers. Like the God of the Hebrew prophets, this God plays favorites, delights in singular contingencies and ironic serendipities. In the Battle of Long Island, fog prolonged the night, allowing Washington's entire army to escape a British trap. This God exercises liberty. He makes choices. He chooses "chosen" peoples and "almost chosen" peoples and loves every people with a love unique to it.

For the seal of the United States the framers chose a motto that derives from Virgil, the Roman poet, but applies better to divine Providence in the biblical sense: *Annuit Coeptis*, "God smiles (approvingly) on our beginnings." If this be Deism, it is a biblical Deism. The God of liberty, like Providence, must love contingency and chance, since only in a universe arrayed in probabilities (not pure necessities) can individual freedom thrive.[13]

My point is not that our founders were on the whole religious men (much less that they were Jewish). My point, rather, is that our founders understood the drama of liberty in a biblical way. It is a mistake to say that they were solely, even predominantly, shaped by the Enlightenment. Of the founders of the French Revolution, that might well be said—but they *passed* by another route.

The American signers thought of liberty in a biblical way—the way men think who are sinners, and know what sinners do—and how we must be checked, and how sentinels to our ambitions must be set in place by the ambitions of every other. "If men were angels," Madison wrote, knowing full well that men are *not* angels, and that the only moral majority that exists is all of us sinners.[14]

The high standards to which God calls a nation composed of Jews and Christians convict us all of sin. That we all are sinners is the elementary finding of biblical religion. That is why any republic built to endure must divide all powers, and as sentries to the common good set proclivity against proclivity, so that a republic of sinners, by sinners, and for sinners shall not perish from this earth.

The framers loved the simple motto: "In God we trust." Its operational meaning is: "For everyone else, checks and balances."

But What Is Liberty?

The signers thought of liberty, then, not as something given but as something learned, and learned only in a *social way* by the weight of an *ethos*; by public vigilance over *habits* and *behaviors*; by education in the *virtues* that make liberty a practice; by books of *exemplars* and *practitioners*; by *heroes*. They honored "moral ecology," holding that culture is prior to, and more basic than, politics or economics. Since culture shapes the habits of the heart, and habits are the tuned engines of our liberty, a polity neglecting them is suicidal. So wrote Samuel Adams in 1775: "For no People will tamely surrender their Liberties, nor can any be easily subdued, when Knowledge is diffused and Virtue is preserved. On the Contrary, when People are universally ignorant, and debauched in their Manners, they will sink under their own Weight without the Aid of foreign Invaders."[15]

The signers, then, thought of liberty as an achievement needing to be learned each day anew. A free people every day takes up responsibilities, with reflection and deliberate choice. But *laws, teachings,* and *official acts* are needed to protect an ethos of virtue, to diminish toxins in the air, and to drive away pollutants.

Equally, the first page of *The Federalist* showed how pivotal one act of liberty may be.

> It seems to have been reserved to the people of this country, by their conduct and example, to decide the important question, whether societies of men are really capable or not of establishing good government from *reflection* and *choice*, or whether they are forever destined to depend for their political constitutions on *accident* and *force*.[16]

Reflection and *choice* are themes the Bible taught our founders. Through their families, they had many years' experience in testing *those* ideas in their own lives. Neither they nor their teachers believed that the lessons of the Bible—or, for that matter, any moral teachings of the past—should lie about unused. Moral teachings should be subjected to experiment in the tests of daily living, proved, absorbed into one's flesh and blood. That is what they meant by traditional virtues. Traditions live by new appropriations ("making one's own") in every generation; otherwise they die.

For the Americans, as Lord Acton saw, liberty is not doing what you wish or what you feel like. Liberty is doing what you ought to do. Dogs and cats have no such choice; they do what instinct urges them to do. Humans are the only animals who have the choice whether or not to obey the higher law of their own nature, whether to follow the better angels of their nature.

Here is the advice the author of the Declaration gave to Peter Carr, a young Virginian who wished to know how to live a life of liberty:

> Give up money, give up fame, give up science, give up the earth itself and all it contains, rather than do an immoral act. And never suppose, that in any possible situation, or under any circumstances, it is best for you to do a dishonorable thing, however slightly so it may appear to you. Whenever you are to do a thing, though it can never be known but to yourself, ask yourself how you would act were all the world looking at you, and act accordingly. Encourage all your virtuous dispositions, and that exercise will make them habitual.[18]

What, then, is human liberty? After reflection and deliberation, to do what you are prepared to commit yourself to, in a way that others may count on. The capacity to practice that sort of liberty the signers called character. A man who acts from deliberation and choice they called a "manly" man. (*Manly* was not a term interchangeable with *male*.)[19] The woman who acts so they called a *valiant* woman. They believed that men and women need help from the surrounding society if enough of them are to act that way. They believed that, whatever may be said of a few of peculiar character, most people need the steel of religion if they are to be tolerably moral.[20]

As adherents to the biblical conception of freedom, the signers were not sure that the American people of 1776 possessed sufficient virtue to bear the costs of war, or after it the long, slow grinding work of peace. John Adams expressed his nagging fear: "I sometimes tremble to think that, although, we are engaged in the best Cause that ever employed the Human Heart, yet the Prospect of success is doubtful not for Want of Power or of Wisdom but of Virtue."[21]

Then, later, Abraham Lincoln warned in 1838 that the memories of the extraordinary virtues that the Revolutionary War taught were being leveled by "the silent artillery of time," as each generation became more remote from the originating spirit of the nation.[22]

What Is Virtue? What Is Character?

What did the signers mean by virtue? They meant habits of self-control, calm reflection, sober consideration of costs and contingencies, courage, and that ability to persevere despite setbacks without which no difficult plan of action can be carried through to completion.[23] In other words, they knew the difference between people who pledge fidelity, chastity, courage, sacrifice, and in general reverence for moral truth, and then do not deliver, and those whose characteristic habits make their words more bankable than bars of gold.

Between a public fit for liberty and one fit for tyranny, good habits make the difference. The name for habits by which men act as slaves is vice.

The signers held three principles: *"No republic without liberty, No liberty without virtue,* and *No virtue* [for most men, in the long run] *without religion."*[24] Of these three, we moderns have weakened on the last two.

These are the principles the signers clung to when they dared to sign their earthshaking Declaration. Contemplating the many solemn oaths of loyalty they had sworn as subjects of the king, counting the costs of the impending war they were now accepting; weighing the consequences of a dreadful act of rebellion on which they would now embark, they pledged their lives, their fortunes, the safety of their families and their homes, and their good names as men who keep their oaths. All these they were prepared to lose, for liberty, if Providence did not permit them to prevail.

The signers taught us what they meant by liberty by what they did and how they did it. Liberty sallies forth amid a troop of virtues, missing any one of which its resolve will surely fail. Benedict Arnold's commitment to liberty failed when one of his inner sentinels slept, perhaps the sentinel that checked his pride.

The Three Meanings of Self-Government

By this path, the Declaration gave the term "self-government" a triple sense. Obviously, the term means a massive shift in form of government, from monarchy to a republic. On a deeper level, self-government means a regime of self-mastery that requires higher virtues than a monarchy.[25] For self-government demands a degree of alertness, self-sacrifice, and responsibility that tests endurance. Obedience to law over time is onerous, and maintaining good habits when the good times roll is tedious. A prior generation may rise to moral heights, and perhaps its sons and daughters will in filial piety maintain that level. But it is not in accord with human nature for later generations to keep that passion burning; it was not so, even in biblical times. "The silent artillery of time" thins out the ranks.

To refill the ranks, virtue must be summoned up. "A Republic can only be supported by pure religion or austere morals," John Adams wrote:

> Public Virtue cannot exist in a nation without private, and public virtue is the only foundation of Republics. There must be a positive Passion for the public good, the public Interest, Honor, Power and Glory, established in the Minds of the People, or there can be no Republican Government, nor any real liberty: and this public passion must be superior to all private Passions.[26]

Why should this be so? Because liberty means acting from reflection and choice, yet often we find deliberation burdensome. Sometimes we *want* to act from passion before we have time to think. Sweet are the uses of perversity.

Michael Novak

The third meaning of "self-government" is this: What in France they turn to *L'État* to do, and what in Sweden they turn to Social Democracy to do, in the United States people turn to each other to do, their own undirected associations. "The first law of democracy," Tocqueville wrote, "is the principle of association."[27]

These are the three meanings of self-government embodied in the Declaration: a republican regime, a moral code of self-mastery, and a capacity for social organization independent of the state. All three enlarge and ennoble ordinary people; make them feel responsible, brave, and free; inspire them to do extraordinary things.

Is It a Declaration Merely of Self-Interest?

A final lesson of the Declaration is more profound. Most scholars give the Declaration a Lockean interpretation by which the fundamental human drive is a premoral principle—self-preservation. So powerful is the war of all against all that we surrender our capacity for violence to the state, and only then does civil society come into being.

Under the Lockean interpretation, each man has an interest in his own freedom but feels no positive calling to end the slavery of others, except by an argument from an enlarged egotism: My safety is more assured in a larger community.[28]

But there is another interpretation—that of Abraham Lincoln. Under Lincoln's view, the need to end slavery is not egotistical but social. No man is an island. Each human is an integral part of one temple, one house. A house divided cannot stand. A house cannot remain half-slave, half-free (and I must add today, half pro-life, half pro-death). Either it will go all for slavery or all for liberty. No man can properly will slavery (or abortion) for himself; hence, not for any other.

Madison, too, in arguing for religious tolerance, noted that creatures of God have duties to God *prior* to the formation of civil society.[29] There is a unity in us, as creatures of one *Creator*, that grounds in us a sense of what is due to others as others, of *what is right*, no matter how we feel about it.[30] This sense obliges us to defend the rights of others, not just our own.

In other words, as Lincoln said, "All honor to Jefferson—to the man who, in the concrete pressure of a struggle for national independence by a single people, had the coolness, forecast and capacity to introduce into a merely revolutionary document, *an abstract truth, applicable to all men and all times,* and so embalm it there, that today, and in all coming days, it shall be a rebuke and a stumbling block to the very harbingers of reappearing tyranny and oppression."[31]

The Declaration holds before us a vision, by which we have vowed to be measured. In the dead of night, as if foreseeing Lincoln's principle, Jefferson wrote: "I tremble for my country when I reflect that God is just."[32] This nation's covenant with the God of liberty cuts its shoulders raw with responsibilities.

The Apple of Gold in the Frame of Silver (Proverbs 25:11)

There is one more point to stress about our founders: their lives, the success of their rebellion, all that they held dear depended on the strength and power of their *union*. If the apple of their eye was liberty, a golden apple, the picture that framed it was the Union.[33]

If the king divided them, they were finished. Among the friends of liberty, there was no room for discord between the South and North, between the most religious and the least so. Everything was done to hold the Union firmly together. Union was the condition of every other good.

To this end, great efforts were made by leading religious preachers such as the president of Princeton, John Witherspoon,[34] and Samuel Cooper, who preached at Harvard for the Inauguration of the Constitution of Massachusetts in 1781,[35] to show the consonance of faith and reason. Faith and reason, they held, are friends, not enemies. Our founders stressed what faith and reason hold in common.

For instance: that it is hard to act with liberty, taking up full responsibility, without sometimes falling and needing to get up again and persevere. Such lessons they found in Plutarch and in Seneca, in Aristotle and in Cicero, as well as in the Book of Kings, and Genesis, and Deuteronomy. In Proverbs they found much that echoed maxims of the Greeks and Romans. From this, they drew much consolation. Their belief in a Creator of all things made it difficult for them to see a separation between the Creator and the laws the Creator placed in nature. They learned from nature willingly, as if it were another book of God.

The union of all citizens, believers and unbelievers, is important as the new millennium begins when, despite the surface calm, our country lies in grievous moral turmoil. Among Americans, some who are not religious and some who are speak as if the other were an alien race. For all of us, it is crucial to see that for America's fundamental principles we have *two* languages, one of reason, one biblical. For our signers, actually, the language of the Bible included the language of reason; the language of reason gave practical force to biblical lessons. That is what Jefferson achieved in the Declaration. Its language is Jewish and biblical, but it is also the language of reason, or close enough to it for the generous mind to make translation easily.

This is the practical point I want to establish. The Declaration ties us all together, nonreligious and religious. "United we stand, divided we fall." That was their motto then. It is still a sound motto.[36]

Our founders did not intend this to be a nation in which Christianity was established as the federal religion. On the other hand, they did establish the principle that every state of the Union *must* have the constitutional form of a republic. And religion, they said often, is indispensable to the survival of republican principles. For instance, George Washington's farewell testament: "Reason and experience both forbid us to expect that national morality can prevail in exclusion of religious principle."[37]

Our founders learned—and taught—a *twofold* language: the language of reason and the language of biblical faith. They did not think that these two languages—at least as regards principles of liberty—were in contradiction. These two languages form a union. The Creator spoke both languages, and so can we. Thus spake the Declaration.

In our time, religious people have made the mistake of thinking that a culture war can be won by political methods. The two—culture and politics—are closely related in certain questions of law. But, mostly, they thrive in different spheres and must be addressed by different methods—even, usually, by different institutions.

Still, a peace between these two groups may demand more of the nonreligious than the religious, may demand more of the first then the second. The nonreligious of today pursue a view that is far too narrow in holding that there is only one valid language, that of reason. In this way, they block their ears to half the music of this nation's founding. They fail to plumb the depths of Lincoln, Washington, or even Jefferson. In the name of tolerance, they themselves have failed to learn one of the two basic languages of many fellow citizens.

We need to repair the union. We all have work to do.

Pessimism? Or Optimism?

Has the culture been lost? Is moral entropy unavoidable? Like Jefferson, we may tremble when we reflect that God is just.

Still, I heard a joke in Poland that I really like, on the difference between the optimist and the pessimist. The pessimist says that things are so bad they can't get any worse. The optimist says, "Oh yes, they can!"

A man I much admire, John Paul II, Karol Wojtyla, has a mordant sense of everything the other side can throw at us—the "culture of death," he calls it, not exactly a cheery prospect. But his favorite admonition is, "Be not afraid."

I heartily approve of his policy prescription, too: *Think* with the pessimists. *Act* with the optimists. "With the pessimists" means without illusion. "With the optimists" means with a firm reliance on divine Providence.

Joseph Warren of Massachusetts stood with the Minutemen at Lexington and took a bullet through his hair above the ear. Two months later, just commissioned a major general in the Continental Army, he learned that fifteen hundred patriots had crept up Bunker Hill at night and silently erected earthen walls. Shocked at daylight to discover this, battalions of Redcoats were assembling for an afternoon attack. Some of them put all of Charlestown to the torch, and tongues of flame from five hundred houses, businesses, and churches leapt into the sky. Joseph Warren rode to Boston and took a position among the fifteen hundred on Bunker Hill.

The American irregulars proved their discipline that day—and the accuracy of huntsmen firing in concentrated bursts. Twice they broke the forward march of thirty-five hundred British troops with fire so withering they blew away as many as 70 to 90 percent of the foremost companies of Redcoats, who lost that day more than a thousand dead. Then the ammunition of the Americans ran out.

While the bulk of the Continental Army retreated, the last units stayed in their trenches to hold off the British hand-to-hand. That is where Major General Joseph Warren was last seen fighting, until a close-range bullet felled him. The British officers had him decapitated.

Freedom is always the most precarious regime. Even a single generation can throw it all away. Every generation must decide.

Joseph Warren had told the men of Massachusetts: "Our country is in danger now, but not to be despaired of. On you depend the fortunes of America. You are to decide the important questions upon which rest the happiness and the liberty of millions not yet born. Act worthy of yourselves."[38]

a single generation can screw everything up

Notes

Erica Carson was especially helpful in preparing the endnotes.

1. "Upon these two foundations, the law of nature and the law of revelation, depend all human laws; that is to say, no human laws should be suffered to contradict these." *Commentaries on the Laws of England*, Vol. 1, Sec. 2 (Chicago: University of Chicago Press, 1979), 8. On the relation between revelation and natural law, see Blackstone's preceding paragraphs.

2. "A Summary View of the Rights of British America, 1774," quoted in *The Life and Selected Writings of Thomas Jefferson*, ed. Adrienne Koch and William Peden (New York: Modern Library, 1972), 11.

3. "When we compare this tone of thought in Europe with the attitude of other civilizations when left to themselves, there seems but one source for its origin. It must come from the medieval insistence on the rationality of God, conceived as with the personal energy of Jehovah and with the rationality of a Greek philosopher. Every detail was supervised and ordered; the search into nature could only result in the vindication of the faith in rationality. Remember that I am not talking of the explicit beliefs of a few individuals. What I mean is the impress on the European mind arising from the unquestioned faith of centuries" Alfred North Whitehead, *Science and the Modern World* (New York: Mentor, 1948), 12-13.

4. David Landes, *The Wealth and Poverty of Nations* (New York: Norton & Company, 1998), 58, where he elaborates on the role of *joie de trouver* in the economic development of the West.

5. Louis Hicks, research for an AEI and Ben Wattenberg television project entitled "The First Measured Century." Another index of U.S. weakness: In 1891, eleven Italian immigrants, cane-workers in New Orleans, were brutally lynched. In protest, the government of Italy withdrew its ambassador. Nativists spread the rumor that Italy would dispatch five iron-hulled battleships to sail along the Eastern seaboard. The entire tonnage of the U.S. Navy did not equal that of even one Italian capital ship. The U.S. Navy lobby vowed that no such potential threat would ever arise again. That was the beginning

of the U.S. "Blue Water Navy," which won the Spanish-American War a decade later. See Richard Gambino, *Vendetta: A True Story of the Worst Lynching in America, the Mass Murder of Italian-Americans in New Orleans in 1891, the Vicious Motivations Behind It, and the Tragic Repercussions that Linger to this Day* (New York: Doubleday, 1977).

6. John Adams to Abigail Adams, quoted in *America's God and Country*, ed. William J. Federer (Coppell, Tex.: FAME Publishing, 1994), 137. I have relied on the Federer account throughout.

7. Consider passages from Acts of Congress in 1779, 1781, and 1782. The Congress thought it proper, for example, "humbly to approach the throne of Almighty God" to ask "that he would establish the independence of these United States upon the basis of religion and virtue." "Thanksgiving Day Proclamation of October 20, 1779," in *The Journals of the Continental Congress 1774-1789*, ed. Worthington C. Ford, Gaillard Hunt, et al. (Washington, D.C.: Government Printing Office, 1904-1937), 15: 1191-92. The following are longer extracts:

> Whereas, it hath pleased Almighty God, the father of mercies, remarkably to assist and support the United States of America in their important struggle for liberty, against the long continued efforts of a powerful nation: it is the duty of all ranks to observe and thankfully acknowledge the interpositions of his Providence in their behalf. Through the whole of the contest, from its first rise to this time, the influence of Divine Providence may be clearly perceived. ["Thanksgiving Day Proclamation of October 26, 1781," ibid., 21:1074-76.]

> It being the indispensable duty of all nations, not only to offer up their supplications to Almighty God, the giver of all good, for his gracious assistance in a time of distress, but also in a solemn and public manner to give him praise for his goodness in general, and especially for great and signal interpositions of his Providence in their behalf; therefore the United States in Congress assembled, taking into their consideration the many instances of divine goodness to these States, in the course of the important conflict in which they have been so long engaged . . . do hereby recommend it to the inhabitants of these States in general, to observe, and request the several States to interpose their authority in appointing and commanding the observation of Thursday, the twenty-eighth day of November next, as a day of solemn thanksgiving to God for all his mercies; and they do further recommend to all ranks and testify their gratitude of God for his goodness, by a cheerful obedience to his laws, and by protecting, each in his station, and by his influence, the practice of true and undefiled religion, which is the great foundation of public prosperity and national happiness. ["Thanksgiving Day Proclamation of October 11, 1782," ibid., 23:647.]

8. The preamble to this resolution reads:

> Whereas, the war in which the United States is engaged with Great Britain, has not only been prolonged, but is likely to be carried to the greatest extremity; and whereas, it becomes all public bodies, as well as private persons, to reverence the Providence of God, and look up to him as the supreme disposer of all events, and the arbiter of the fate of nations. ["Fast Day Proclamation of December 11, 1776," ibid., 21:1074-76.]

9. *Federalist* Nos. 20, 38, 43. From France, Alexis de Tocqueville also took up this theme: "The gradual development of the principle of equality is a providential fact. It has all the chief characteristics of such a fact: it is universal, it is durable, it constantly eludes all human interference, and all events as well as all men contribute to its progress." *De-*

mocracy in America, Vol. I, Henry Reeve text as revised by Francis Bowen, ed. Phillips Bradley (New York: Vintage Books, 1945), xi.

10. Pauline Maier, *American Scripture: Making the Declaration of Independence* (New York: Knopf, 1997).

11. Richard Hooker offers a taxonomy of the many meanings of *eternal law* and *natural law* in use for centuries: "I am not ignorant that by 'law eternal' the learned for the most part do understand the order, not which God hath eternally purposed himself in all his works to observe, but rather that which with himself he hath set down as expedient to be kept by all his creatures, according to the several conditions wherewith he hath endowed them. . . . Now that law which, as it is laid up in the bosom of God, they call *Eternal*, receiveth according unto the different kinds of things which are subject unto it different and sundry kinds of names. That part of it which ordereth natural agents we call usually *Nature's law*; that which Angels do clearly behold and without any swerving observe is a law *Celestial* and heavenly; the law of *Reason*, that which bindeth creatures reasonably in this world, and with which by reason that may most plainly perceive themselves bound; that which bindeth them, and is not known but by special revelation from God, *Divine* law; *Human* law, that which out of the law either of reason or of God men probably gathering to be expedient, they make it a law. All things therefore, which are as they ought to be, are conformed unto *this second law eternal*; and even those things which to this eternal law are not conformable are notwithstanding in some sort ordered by *the first eternal law*. . . . Wherefore to come to the law of nature; albeit thereby we sometimes mean that manner of working which God hath set for each created thing to keep; yet forasmuch as those things are termed most properly natural agents, which keep the law of their kind unwittingly, as the heavens and elements of the world, which can do no otherwise than they do; and forasmuch as we give unto intellectual natures the name of Voluntary agents, that so we may distinguish them from the other; expedient it will be, that we sever the law of nature observed by the one from that which the other is tied unto." Richard Hooker, *Ecclesiastical Polity*, Book I, (Great Britain: Carcanet Press, 1990), 40-41.

12. Algernon Sidney, *Discourses Concerning Government*, ed. Thomas G. West (Indianapolis: Liberty Fund, 1996); Thomas West's introduction, xxiii.

13. On the concept of emergent probability, see Michael Novak, *The Spirit of Democratic Capitalism* (Lanham, Md.: Madison Books, 1991), 71-81 and Bernard Lonergan, *Insight: A Study of Human Understanding* (New York: Longman's, 1957), chapter VIII, sections 5 and 6.

14. *Federalist* No. 51: "In framing a government which is to be administered by men over men, the great difficulty lies in this: you must first enable the government to control the governed; and in the next place oblige it to control itself. A dependence on the people is, no doubt the primary control on the government; but experience has taught mankind the necessity of auxiliary precautions." *The Federalist Papers* (New York: New American Library, 1961).

15. Samuel Adams to James Warren, November 4, 1775, *The Founders' Constitution*, Vol. I, ed. Phillip Kurland and Ralph Lerner (Chicago: University of Chicago Press: 1987), 668.

16 *Federalist* No. 1.

17. Lord Acton's famous formulation is "Liberty is not doing what one wishes; liberty is doing what one ought." Also, "Liberty and Morality: How they try to separate them, to found liberty on rights, on enjoyments, not on duties. Insist on their identity. Liberty is the condition which makes it easy for Conscience to govern. Liberty is government of Conscience. Reign of Conscience." Quoted in "Liberty," *Essays in Religion,*

Politics, and Morality, Vol. III, ed. J. Rufus Fears (Indianapolis: Liberty Classics, 1985), 491-92.

18. Jefferson adds a few lines later: "Nothing is so mistaken as the supposition, that a person is to extricate himself from a difficulty, by intrigue, by chicanery, by dissimulation, by trimming, by an untruth, by an injustice. This increases the difficulties ten fold; and those who pursue these methods, get themselves so involved at length, that they can turn no way but their infamy becomes more exposed. It is of great importance to set a resolution, not to be shaken, never to tell an untruth. There is no vice so mean, so pitiful, so contemptible; and he who permits himself to tell a lie once, finds it much easier to do it a second and third time, till at length it becomes habitual; he tells lies without attending to it, and truths without the world's believing him. This falsehood of the tongue leads to that of the heart, and in time depraves all its good dispositions." See "Letter to Peter Carr, August 19, 1785," in *Thomas Jefferson: Writings* (New York: The Library of America, 1984), 814-15.

19. See Harvey Mansfield's Bradley Lecture, "Is Manliness a Virtue?" October 14, 1997, available on The American Enterprise Website: www.aei.org.

20. "Whatever may be conceded to the influence of refined education on minds of peculiar structure, reason, and experience both forbid us to expect that national morality can prevail in exclusion of religious principle." George Washington, "Farewell Address," *George Washington: A Collection,* ed. W. B. Allen (Indianapolis: Liberty Classics, 1988), 521-22.

21. John Adams to Mercy Warren, April 16, 1776, op. cit., 670.

22. "Address to the Young Men's Lyceum of Springfield, Illinois," *Abraham Lincoln: Speeches and Writings 1832-1858,* Vol. 1, ed. Don Fehrenbacher (New York: Library of America, 1989), 29-36.

23. On this part, cf. Christopher DeMuth's unpublished paper, "Remarks at AEI Chairman's Dinner," 10 December 1998. See also George Will, "The Primacy of Culture," *Newsweek,* U.S. Edition, (The Last Word, 18 January 1999): 64.

24. Jeffrey Morrison, "John Witherspoon on 'The Public Interest of Religion,'" unpublished paper prepared for presentation at the John Courtney seminar, American Enterprise Institute, 16 February 1999, 18.

25. "For my own part I am so tasteless as to prefer a Republic, if We must erect an independent Government in America, which you know is utterly against my Inclination. But a Republic, although it will infallibly beggar me and my Children, will produce Strength, Hardiness, Activity, Courage, Fortitude, and Enterprise; the manly noble and Sublime Qualities in human Nature, in Abundance. A Monarchy would probably, somehow or other make me rich, but it would produce so much Taste and Politeness, so much Elegance in Dress, Furniture, Equipage, so much Musick and Dancing, so much Fencing and Skaiting, so much Cards and Backgammon; so much Horse Racing and Cockfighting, so many Balls and Assemblies, so many Plays and Concerts that the very Imagination of them makes me feel vain, light, frivolous, and insignificant." John Adams to Mercy Warren, January 8, 1776, *The Founders' Constitution,* 669.

26. Adams, *Founders' Constitution.*

27. *Democracy in America,* 189.

28. "Jefferson's horizon, with its grounding in Locke, saw all commands to respect the rights of others as fundamentally hypothetical imperatives: *if* you do not wish to be a slave, then refrain from being a master. Lincoln agreed, but he also said in substance: he who wills freedom for himself must simultaneously will freedom for others. . . . Because all men by nature have an equal right to justice, all men have an equal duty to do justice."

Harry Jaffa, *The Crisis of the House Divided* (Chicago: University of Chicago Press, 1959), 326.

29. "It is the duty of every man to render to the Creator such homage, and such only, as he believes to be acceptable to him. This duty is precedent, both in order of time and degree of obligation, to the claims of civil society. Before any man can be considered as a member of civil society, he must be considered as a subject of the Governor of the universe." James Madison, "Memorial and Remonstrance Against Religious Assessments," Amendment I, No. 43, quoted in *The Founders' Constitution*, Vol. I, 82.

30. "The concept of *what is right* is the concept of an objective condition, a condition discernible by reason. 'All I ask for the negro is that if you do not like him, let him alone,' said Lincoln with a pathos which anticipates the war years. But his meaning is that the test of right is not how something agrees with our passions but how it agrees with a discernment of what is due to a man. Right conceived as subjective passion does *not* forbid us to do what is objectively wrong; it only directs us to do whatever we deem necessary for *our* lives and *our* liberty. Right conceived as a state or condition in which every man is rendered his due forbids us to dissociate the value to ourselves of our own lives and liberties and the value to themselves of the lives and liberties of any men who may be affected by our actions." Jaffa, op. cit., 329.

31. Letter to Henry L. Pierce and Others, April 6, 1859, *Abraham Lincoln: Speeches and Writings,* New York: 1859-1865 (New York: Library of America, 1989), 19.

32. To this famous sentence, Jefferson also added: "I think a change already perceptible, since the origin of the present revolution. The spirit of the master is abating, that of the slave rising from the dust, his condition mollifying, the way I hope preparing, under the auspices of heaven, for a total emancipation, and that this is disposed, in the order of events, to be with the consent of the masters, rather than by their extirpation." Notes on the State of Virginia," in *Thomas Jefferson: Writings,* ed. Merrill D. Peterson (New York: Library of America, 1984), 289. These sentences indicate that Jefferson, too, saw the Declaration as an ideal already working in history.

33. "The assertion of that *principle*, at *that time*, was the word, '*fitly spoken*,' which has proved an 'apple of gold' to us. *The Union*, and the *Constitution*, are the picture of silver, subsequently framed around it." Abraham Lincoln, fragment: "The Constitution and the Union" [1860], *Abraham Lincoln: His Speeches and Writings*, ed. Roy Basler (New York: World Publishing, 1946), 513.

34. "If your cause is just—you may look with confidence to the Lord and intreat [sic] him to plead it as his own. You are all my witnesses, that this is the first time of my introducing any political subject into the pulpit. At this season, however, it is not only lawful but necessary, and I willingly embrace the opportunity of declaring my opinion without any hesitation, that the cause in which America is now in arms is the cause of justice, of liberty, and of human nature. So far as we have hitherto proceeded, I am satisfied that the confederacy of the colonies has not been the effect of pride, resentment, or sedition, but of a deep and general conviction, that our civil and religious liberties, and consequently in a great measure the temporal and eternal happiness of us and our posterity, depended on the issue. The knowledge of God and his truths have from the beginning of the world been chiefly, if not entirely, confined to those parts of the earth, where some degree of liberty and political justice were to be seen. . . . There is not a single instance in history in which civil liberty was lost, and religious liberty preserved entire. If therefore we yield up our temporal property, we at the same time deliver the conscience into bondage." John Witherspoon, "The Dominion of Providence over the Passions of Men," quoted in Ellis Sandoz, *Political Sermons of the American Founding Era, 1730-1805* (Indianapolis: Liberty Press, 1991), 529-59.

35. "We want not, indeed, a special revelation from heaven to teach us that men are born equal and free; that no man has a natural claim of dominion over his neighbors, nor one nation any such claim upon another. . . . These are the plain dictates of that reason and common sense with which the common parent of men has informed the human bosom. It is, however, a satisfaction to observe such everlasting maxims of equity confirmed, and impressed upon the consciences of men, by the instructions, precepts, and examples given us in the sacred oracles." Samuel Cooper, "Sermon on the Day of the Commencement of the Constitution" [1780], ibid., 627-57.

36. Between the religious and the nonreligious the relation is not symmetrical. For the nonreligious, it may be difficult to use religious language. For the religious, it is a quite familiar move to recur to the language of reason, a move often endorsed in the religious tradition. For the religious, one additional reason for trusting reason is that the Creator created it as well. Some of the nonreligious trust reason, but these days many do not.

37. Op. cit., p. 522. William Bennett collects several of these texts in *Our Sacred Honor* (New York: Simon and Schuster, 1997). Another source is James Hutson, *Religion and the Founding of the American Republic*, Conference at the Library of Congress, 19 June 1998 (Lanham, Md.: Rowman & Littlefield, 1999).

38. Quoted in Ronald Reagan's "First Inaugural Address," January 20, 1981, *Speaking My Mind: Selected Speeches* (New York: Simon & Schuster, 1989), 64. Regarding Joseph Warren's role at Bunker Hill, I have learned much from Catherine Drinker Bowen, *John Adams and the American Revolution* (Boston: Little, Brown & Company, 1950); David Ramsay, *The History of the American Revolution*, ed. Lester H. Cohen (first published 1789; Indianapolis: Liberty Classics, 1990); Benson Bobrick, *Angel in the Whirlwind* (New York: Simon & Schuster, 1997).

Part II

Unto Caesar and Unto God

Chapter 4

Religion and American Democracy

Jean Bethke Elshtain

Alexis de Tocqueville did not miss much during his tour of America, a mission that yielded his nineteenth-century masterwork, *Democracy in America*. Although he failed to pick up the often extraordinary energies of American evangelism—his reaction to what he considered such frenzy being the following: "From time to time strange sects arise which endeavor to strike out extraordinary paths to eternal happiness. Religious insanity is very common in the United States"[1]—he *did* see how thoroughly religion and politics were saturated with one another. American democracy from the beginning was premised on the enactment of projects that were a complex intermingling of religious and political imperatives. The majority of Americans were religious seekers and believers who saw in communal liberty the freedom to *be* religious rather than freedom *from* religion. It is, therefore, not surprising that such a huge chunk of American juridical life has been devoted to sorting out the often ineptly named church-state debate. In a less churched society, this would be a far less salient issue.

But what does our profession of belief—some 95 percent of Americans claim belief in God and fully 70 percent membership in a church, synagogue, or mosque[2]—really mean? How does it play itself out on the ground, so to speak? Here a bit of backdrop is helpful in order that we might better situate and explore the vagaries of the present moment.

The West is perhaps unique in this regard, namely, that it has never been hospitable to theocracy, a fusion of, or nondistinction between, the political and the religious. Religion is not only established in theocracies, it dominates politics as in contemporary fundamentalist Islamic states in which mullahs also run the government. There were often close alliances in the history of the West between throne and altar, to be sure. But this is not the same thing. In other words, a differentiation between politics and religion was sown in Western culture from very early on, quite pointedly so with the coming of Christianity. Christians asked: What has Christ to do with Caesar? The answer varied widely. Too, the church, and the synagogue before it and ongoingly, embodied an alternative

39

politics, having their own understandings of community membership, authority, rule, and the nature of the kingdom. The central distinction marked in medieval papal doctrine was that between *regnum* and *sacerdotium*, roughly marking the swords of the earthly kingdom and the spiritual kingdom respectively. The two got all tangled up with one another, to be sure, but they were nonetheless distinct. The spiritual sword was held to be superior because it gestured beyond the immediate realm to the eternal. But the secular sword had its own dignity, its own autonomy and purposes. It could, however, be called to account by the sacred realm, by those who wielded the spiritual sword on behalf of the city of God on earthly pilgrimage. The nations were under judgment and not wholly autonomous in all things.

The post-medieval history of the West is a story of various comings-together and, finally, definitively, teasing apart of church and state. But religion and politics are something else. These simply cannot be separated. Too much of the same territory is claimed by each. Consider American democracy, then. We begin from the beginning with no establishment of religion but with free exercise of religion. Bear in mind as well that the views of a few of the great founders of this republic were somewhat anomalous, Jefferson first and foremost, who famously claimed that it mattered not whether his neighbor believed in no God or twenty gods; it neither picked his pocket nor broke his leg. The vast majority of Americans, then and now, were not nearly so agnostic about their neighbors' beliefs.

It is utterly unsurprising, then, that when Tocqueville toured America in the Jacksonian era he wrote of the ways in which religion in the United States, by which he primarily meant Christianity in its various incarnations including Catholicism, both generated and made use of democratic instincts; religion helped to shape the mores, the habits of the heart. Tocqueville further observed that settled beliefs about God and human nature were indispensable in the conduct of daily life—you simply could not function if you woke up every morning and had to determine what truths would guide you over the next twenty-four hours— and that, in general, when a people's religion is destroyed, it enervates and prepares them not for liberation, but for bondage.

This is, of course, an extraordinarily complex story and an often bewildering one, especially for foreign observers. So let's add a few more Tocquevillian bits. Remember that, for Tocqueville, America embodied a coming age of democracy and equality. One could not understand the great movement toward equality without understanding the Christian insistence that all are equal in the eyes of God. This equality, enacted politically, brings great benefits, but it also opens the door to certain dangerous tendencies. Democratic egalitarianism tends to isolate people from one another as we all, as competing individuals, go in quest of the "same" thing. We become strivers and isolate ourselves one from the other. Here religion is vital as a chastening influence as it inspires contrary urges by drawing people into community and away from narrow materialism. Religion, in Tocqueville's words, helps to "purify, control, and restrain that excessive and exclusive taste for well-being human beings acquire in an age of equality."[3]

Religion contributes to the maintenance of a democratic republic by directing the mores and helping, thereby, to regulate political life. Tocqueville insisted that the ideas of Christianity and liberty are so completely intermingled that if you tried to sever religion from democracy in America, you would wind up destroying democracy. Democracy needs the sort of transcendent justification that religion helps to provide; thus, the eighteenth-century philosophers were wrong about the weakening of religion. "It is tiresome," notes Tocqueville ironically, "that the facts do not fit their theory at all."[4] For, surprisingly, the separation of church and state in America had led to an astonishingly religious atmosphere. By diminishing the *official* power of religion, Americans had enhanced its social strength. Perhaps, deep down, Americans understood that religion feeds hope and is thus attached to a constitutive principle of human nature. Amidst the flux and tumult of a rambunctious democratic politics, religion shaped and mediated the passions. Were the days to come when those passions got unleashed upon the world unrestrained, then we would arrive at an unhappy moment indeed, a dreary world of democratic despotism.

For there were at least two great dangers threatening the existence of religion (and indirectly, democracy) according to Tocqueville, namely, schism and indifference. Schism pits us against one another in suspicion and enmity; indifference invites us not to care about one another at all. Were Tocqueville around today, I believe he would point to both and he would worry that we are in danger of losing that generous concern for others that religion, in institutionally robust forms, not "spirituality" in vaporous individualist forms, promotes. As well, operating from some common moral basis, which does not require doctrinal leveling but does demand searching for certain core norms we share, helps people learn how to compromise because they agree on so many important things.

If we slide into a world of schism, a world in which differences become the occasion for isolation, we lose authentic pluralism which requires institutional bases from which to operate. It is pluralism that gives us the space to be both American and Protestant, Catholic, Jew, Muslim, on and on. Absent robust and vibrant faith and civic institutions, we are thrown back on our own devices; we lose the strength that membership provides; we forget that we can know a good in common that we cannot know alone. Should we arrive at this Tocquevillian impasse, we would find that individuals, striving to stand upright in the winds blowing from centers of governmental or economic power now operating minus that chastening influence from other vital sources, would soon be flattened. People would grow apart and become strangers one to another. We might still have kin, but we would no longer have a country in the sense of a polity of which we were essential parts.

This is where a form of dogmatic skepticism, corrosive of all belief, enters. Tocqueville knew that people would always question and challenge. But what happens if there is nothing but skepticism of a dogmatic sort that is unable to sustain any beliefs. Don't you think Tocqueville would see that we Americans at the beginning of this new century might be in this danger zone as well? In our desire to be sophisticated, in our determination to be nobody's fools, we may well and truly be undermining our ability to believe and to affirm anything at all save the ephemeral ground of our own subjective experience.

So where are we at this point? What do we see when we look around? First, we see a smorgasbord religiosity whose primary aim seems to be to make us feel good about God, but God forbid that this should place any demands on us. Second, as a corollary, we see what might be called a hollowing out or deinstitutionalization of religion in many quarters, a loss of institutional robustness. This creates a real problem as faith absent strong institutions cannot be sustained over time; religious life becomes all fission and fragment absent framing rules and doctrines and underlying beliefs. Here *we* stand.

A deinstitutionalized, feel-good religiosity cannot carry out the tasks of formation Tocqueville found so central in forging a sturdy, decent, self-governing American character. If religion is just another voluntary association, it is not religion any more in a strong sense. This puts us in danger of losing the connection between freedom and truth. For freedom is not just me maximizing my preferences, as some who favor market models hold, but is tethered to truth as a part of our very being, our inner constitution. Freedom, rightly understood, which is always a chastened notion of freedom, frees us *for* solidarity with others. An authentic view of freedom—understood in and through the prism of relationality, of brotherhood and sisterhood—must challenge misguided views that undermine authentic freedom. But without certain formative institutions we cannot sustain freedom in the authentic sense. We enter a danger zone in which our differences, which should be great blessings, as Francis Cardinal George, archbishop of Chicago, has argued, become instead destructive divisions. Our great religious traditions offer hope and solace, the promise of a community of the faithful. One's Internet chat room is not quite the same thing.

I want to be careful here because I would not want to leave the impression that I believe religion performs certain useful functions and that is its ultimate and most defensible aim and purpose. No, instead, the aim of religion is to bear us toward the truth—to direct our very beings toward a conformity with true freedom as relationality, as communion, grounded always in the dignity of persons. Religion opens us to the God in whose likeness we were created. In the words of the great Saint Augustine, "Thou hast made us to thyself and our hearts are restless til they rest in Thee."[5] And this restlessness—"everybody's got a hungry heart" sings Bruce Springsteen—channeled and made ever fresh through religious belief, helps us to face and to try to make whole a wounded world.[6] But this mission of religion may be blocked, oddly enough, nowadays in the name of religious freedom or tolerance.

Let me explain what I mean. In a recent book by the distinguished sociologist, Alan Wolfe, *One Nation, After All*, Wolfe describes what he calls a modern religious tolerance in a discussion entitled "Morality Writ Small." Wolfe's middle-class respondents—and the vast majority of Americans are middle-class and understand themselves through this lens—see religion as a private matter to be discussed only reluctantly. This departs in quite dramatic ways from a deeper, richer understanding of what tolerance is or what it requires, for one thing. And, for another, it suggests that many of our fellow citizens have come to believe that to endorse a properly secular state that has no established ties to any religious institution means one is obliged to support a secularized society in which religion is reduced to a purely private role. Not so. Yet this is precisely what so many of the respondents in this important book seem to be saying they want. So much for William Lloyd Garrison, Dorothy Day, Martin Luther King Jr., and a small army of other great citizens who did not embrace this nicety!

Professor Wolfe sees his respondents as trying to be welcoming to all faiths. His Mrs. Tompkins—one of the people interviewed in the book—thinks that one way to ease the rough edges off religious conviction is to refuse to accept any particular "dogma whole" as if the doctrines or teachings of various faith communities were arbitrary impositions rather than worked out and complex teachings that took shape over centuries. Instead, she continues, one should just "live with the concept of God as you perceive it."[7] Is this not a form of terminal subjectivism? If it is all up to you, a community of belief is lost and we slide into indifference.

But something even more troubling seems to be going on. There is a deep undercurrent of fearfulness running just beneath the surface of the words of so many of the middle-class Americans in Professor Wolfe's book. They seem to have struck a tacit bargain with themselves that goes like this: If I am quiet about what I believe and everybody else is quiet about what he or she believes, then nobody will interfere with the rights of anybody else. But this is precisely what real believers, whether political or religious or both, cannot do: keep quiet—whether believers in Martin Luther King's beloved community, or in ending the war in Vietnam on justice grounds derived from religious conviction, or in opposing the current abortion regime for similar reasons. To tell political religious believers to shut up for they will interfere with my rights by definition simply by speaking out is an intolerant idea. It is, in effect, to tell folks that they cannot really believe what they believe or be who they are. Don't ask; don't tell.

What fears underwrite this attitude? One, surely, is of religious intolerance, even religious warfare, though, of course, if you were to do a body count, the murderous antireligious ideologies of the twentieth century would win that prize hands down. But the fear now seems to extend to public expression itself. Wolfe notes that his respondents are disturbed when religion is taken out of the private realm. But a private religion is no religion at all. One must have the public expression of faith for it to be faith, and public expression is not forcing anything on anybody. But, to those interviewed for *One Nation, After All,* that in and of itself—public expression—seems to cross a line because you are supposed to keep quiet about what you believe most strongly. If you do not, it may require of me that I actually enter into an act of discernment—What do I think about what you are claiming?—and that many Americans do not want to do.

[handwritten marginalia:]
some think religion should be a private matter.
the secular leaders think it's essential to incorporate religion into gov.
keep people have their beliefs isn't tolerance.

[handwritten notes at bottom:]
- religion is suppose to be public
- not right to make religion private
- making it public makes Americans challenge their beliefs.

There are, of course, certain virtues here imbedded: Don't rush to judgment; live and let live. But I want to focus on the vices. Although Wolfe describes the demand for privatization as a tolerant one flowing from a desire to be "inclusive" and "nonabsolutist," I wonder. Many of his respondents do seem quite absolutist—about everybody shutting up. Consider the remarks of Jody Fields: "If you are a Hindu and you grew up being a Hindu, keep it to yourself. Don't impose your religion, and don't make me feel bad because I do this and you do this."[8] Surely this is not tolerance at all but extraordinary intolerance of religious pluralism. If one changes Hindu to Jew in the comment, that becomes stunningly clear. So when we are told that "keep it to yourself" presages a "period of increasing religious pluralism,"[9] I would say, "hardly." Telling a Hindu to hide being a Hindu is scarcely a picture of robust pluralism.

Now some respondents in *One Nation, After All* do seem to be authentic religious pluralists, more generous in their attitudes. Here, for example, is Cathy Ryan, perturbed because Christmas carols cannot be sung anymore in the public schools of her town at Christmas time because Muslims may get upset. Her response: "Well, excuse me, but let's teach Muslim songs too—don't wipe out all culture, add to it. Do Hannukkah songs. Let's find out what a dreidel represents. Let's find out what Muslims do."[10] This is real tolerance, I would submit, of a sort that encourages the public expression and representation of differences with the view that we are all enriched through the process. As Pope John Paul II always tells us: "Be not afraid!" Cathy Ryan is open to robust pluralism. And one might argue that it is in America that such forms of "trans-nationality" (as the great proponent and critic of early twentieth-century progressivism, Randolph Bourne, called it) have found and continue to find relatively benign expression.

Legal scholar Michael McConnell, in a paper on "Believers as Equal Citizens," reminds us of several different versions of Jewish emancipation historically. One expected Jews to disappear as a distinctive group once they were given their civil rights. Under the terms of Jewish emancipation in France, for example, Jews were expected to give up civil aspects of Talmudic law, to disavow any political implications of their faith, to abandon altogether the use of Yiddish, and to relinquish their semi-autonomous communal institutions. This by contrast to American pluralism. Writes McConnell:

> The great public feast given in 1789 in Philadelphia, then the nation's capitol, to celebrate ratification of the Constitution included a fitting symbol of this new pluralistic philosophy: the feast included a special table where the food conformed to Jewish dietary laws. This was a fitting symbol because it included Jewish Americans in the celebration without requiring that they sacrifice their distinctiveness as Jews. By contrast, in France Napoleon summoned the leaders of the Jewish community to a "Great Sanhedrin," where he insisted that the Jewish law be modified to enable the Jewish people to be integrated into the French nation. In a gesture no less revealing than the kosher table in Philadelphia, Napoleon's Minister of the Interior scheduled the first session to be held on Saturday. Here we see three alternatives. Under the *ancien regime*, Jews would be excluded from the celebration, for they could not be citizens. Under

the secular state, Jews would be welcome to attend, but they would be expected to eat the same food that other citizens eat. If they want to keep kosher, they should do it at home, in private, at their own expense. Under the pluralist vision, multiple tables are provided to ensure that for Protestants, it is a Protestant country, for Catholics a Catholic country [for Muslims, a Muslim country], and the Jew, if he [or she] pleases, may establish in it his [or her] New Jerusalem.[11]

So let us not worry so much about conflict or difference that we deny pluralism its forms of public expression—for this is the only way, really, that we have of learning about the gifts others have to offer. There is a difference between "keep it to yourself" and tolerance. In the words of Stephen Carter: "Tolerance is not simply a willingness to listen to what others have to say. It is also a resistance to the quick use of state power . . . to force dissenters and the different to conform."[12] If we do not allow religious dissenters to display their beliefs as public moral critics, in their own voices, then it is we who are intolerant.

Now let us draw politics and religion together one more time. Political commentator E. J. Dionne has written that Americans are fed up with politics and many among us just want politics to go away. The majority of middle-class Americans in *One Nation, After All* also seem to want real religious conviction to go away, too, especially in light of their distrust of "organized religion," as if there were any other kind. I want to suggest that contemporary distrust of organized politics and organized religion goes hand in hand. Both involve public expression, collectivities of persons involved in a shared enterprise, rules and convictions, and sometimes hard-hitting encounters. That we seem not to have the stomach for either suggests our capacity for democracy itself is growing ever more anemic. A distaste for conflict is a distaste for politics. The great Frederick Douglass once remarked that you cannot have rain without occasional thunder and lightning. Yet that is what so many of us seem to want: spring showers, lovely gardens, but no thunderstorms. Need I note that life does not work like that and that no complex democratic politics can survive if we go underground with what we care about most deeply.

To me this suggests that we are not doing a very good job of social and political and, yes, religious formation: preparing people for a world in which there are disagreements and there are decisions to be made and one cannot always tell the Hindus to keep it to themselves.

This draws us, at last, to certain basic questions. Who are we anyhow? In what does the good of human beings consist? How can we come to recognize, to honor, and to cultivate that good in wisdom and in truth? In two films of the great American director, John Ford, a shocked outsider puts fundamental questions. Consider "My Darling Clementine"[13] when Henry Fonda as Wyatt Earp, who has given up his badge and left Dodge City with his brothers to try to create a new life, enters a town for a shave and finds people fleeing in horror and screaming as a drunk shooter lays waste to the place and law enforcement officials flinch and throw down their badges because they are not getting paid enough for such really dangerous duty. "What kind of a town is this?" queries Fonda in amazement.

In the opening of "Who Shot Liberty Valence?,"[14] Jimmy Stewart, as lawyer Rance Stoddard, is riding in a coach into Shinbone to start a new life in the West when the stagecoach is robbed and the local villain, Liberty Valence—who takes all sorts of liberties until those who struggle to create a settled civil society, to build churches and schools and political institutions, triumph—steals a brooch off a lady's garment although she pleads, "Please take everything else, but not that, it was a gift from my late husband," and Stewart, who doesn't carry a gun and is surrounded by armed desperadoes, cries out: "What kind of a man are you?" An aim of religion is to help us, with God's help, to ask and struggle to answer those questions: What kind of a place is this? What kind of people are we?

Notes

1. Alexis de Tocqueville, *Democracy in America* (New York: Alfred A. Knopf, 1994), Book II, Chapter 12, 134.

2. Gallup polling data. www.gallup.com/poll/indicators/indreligion.asp (April 1998).

3. Tocqueville, *Democracy*, 448.

4. Tocqueville, *Democracy*, 295.

5. *The Confessions of St. Augustine*, trans. F. J. Sheed (New York: Sheed & Ward, 1942), 3.

6. "Hungry Heart" by Bruce Springsteen. Copyright © 1980 by Bruce Springsteen (ASCAP). Reprinted by permission.

7. Alan Wolfe, *One Nation, After All* (New York: Penguin Books, 1998), 51.

8. Wolfe, *One Nation*, 63.

9. Wolfe, *One Nation*, 64.

10. Wolfe, *One Nation*, 70.

11. Michael McConnell, "Believers as Equal Citizens" (Law and Interpretation Section Panel, Association of American Law Schools National Meeting, Washington, D.C., January 1997).

12. Stephen L. Carter, *The Dissent of the Governed: A Meditation on Law, Religion, and Loyalty* (Cambridge, Mass: Harvard University Press, 1998), 85.

13. *My Darling Clementine*, dir. John Ford, 97 min. (20th Century Fox, 1946).

14. *The Man Who Shot Liberty Valance*, dir. John Ford, 123 min. (Paramount Pictures, 1962).

Religion and Politics in America: Faith, Culture, and Strategic Choices, Robert Booth Fowler and Allen D. Hertzke (Boulder, Colo.: Westview Press A Division of Harper Collins Publisher, Inc., 1995), 129.

Chapter 5

Religion and Public Life

James Q. Wilson

Religion makes a large difference in the lives of millions of Americans despite the fact that American government is indifferent to its existence and hostile to its support. This may only appear to be a paradox. In fact, religion may be important here in part because governmental indifference allows so many religions to prosper. Voltaire predicted this in the eighteenth century when he observed that a nation with one religion has oppression, a nation with two has civil war, and a nation with a hundred has peace. Much the same argument was made by Adam Smith.

> Though this is a nation inhabited by people from other countries where religious observance is less important than it is here, the law and culture that sustains multiple sects has worked its effect on many who have arrived here, giving them a chance to form and organize around their own beliefs, to create and sustain their own churches, and to proclaim and defend their own visions. America enjoys religious freedom, and, accordingly, many religions have prospered. Freedom of religious expression has not stunted religion; it has encouraged it.[1]

It has especially encouraged the kind of religion that is often called fundamentalist. Churches that, by their own beliefs, feel it necessary to reach out and organize others—churches, that is, in which the missionary impulse is particularly strong—are the ones that most benefit from religious freedom. Missionary churches are dependent for their survival on the people whom they can convert, and so they are the ones that are most likely to reflect the wants and needs of ordinary people. More traditional churches, with little missionary impulse, are at a disadvantage: They will often find their numbers dwindling because they have no serious impulse to increase those numbers. Put simplistically, a traditional church is one to which its normal members repair when getting married or buried but to which they rarely give their regular attention. A fundamentalist church, by contrast, is one that can only exist if it succeeds in drawing to it

47

people for whom religion makes a daily difference. Fundamentalist churches not only benefit from religious liberty, they contribute to it. David Hume explained why. Those religions that rely on what he called "enthusiasm"—that is, on religion that embraces rapture and a belief in direct and divine illumination—lead to more furious passions but in time to greater civil liberty. The reason, Hume suggested, is that enthusiasm is both the enemy of hierarchical churches and an expression of animated people who cherish liberty.[2] What we now call a fundamentalist church—one that believes that people can acquire a direct knowledge of God without priestly direction—depends on the religious equivalent of the entrepreneurial spirit, just as a small business person, unlike the politically more powerful large corporation, depends on economic freedom.

For these reasons, and for others I do not yet understand, religious observance is more common in the United States than in many other industrialized nations even though this country was settled by people from the very nations where such observances are less customary.

This great force in American life makes a difference in human life. This is a matter to which scholars have given relatively little attention because scholars, especially in the humanities and the social sciences, are disproportionately drawn from the ranks of people who are indifferent—or even hostile—to religion. But if a creed did not make some difference, far fewer people would embrace it.

Religion affects morality, but not in the way many people suppose. Let me repeat here an argument made more clearly and fully by Michael Oakeshott.[3] Religion cannot, I think, be either the source of morality or provide the support for morality. It cannot be the source because it is obvious that there are highly moral people who are not religious and fanatical extremists who are deeply religious. In every nation there are many moral people who have few or weak religious views and act morally without reference to a religious doctrine. Occasionally, an entire nation seems unreligiously moral. Japan is often held up, rightly, as a nation that is remarkably free of the worst excesses of crime, drug abuse, and political violence, yet Japan has achieved this record, one that cannot be duplicated by any other advanced industrial nation, without much that resembles religious commitment. Religion is rarely, even in its sermons and writings, a true source of morality. When Jesus told us of the Golden Rule, he was not telling us anything we had not known before; he was only reminding us that, though we knew this rule, we were often violating it. As Samuel Johnson was later to put it, people need to be reminded more often than they need to be instructed.

Nor is it the case that religion provides the main sanction for a moral code. Many people believe that the natural life of humans cannot supply a guide to human action. If we think that by contemplating who we are and how society is organized we can find a principle of right conduct, we commit what some have called the naturalistic fallacy. This problem leads many to believe that human nature is so devoid of moral sentiments that any moral code of action must require divine revelation. We are then induced to obey that code out of either a desire to please the God that supplied it or out of a desire to avoid the threat of eternal damnation or to acquire otherworldly pleasures.

The desire to please God is a worthy one, but it is not clear that pleasing the commands of a superior force is sufficient to define an act as moral. This would be equivalent to acting morally because we wish to please a friend. This is not an unworthy motive and is indeed the source of much moral behavior but it does raise a question: Does moral action require subordination to another party? Perhaps to some extent, but not to every extent. Morality entirely defined as obedience to a superior being becomes identical to blind obedience. It suggests that morality depends on obedience even though many people make moral choices without such obedience. They make those choices because the so-called naturalistic fallacy is itself a fallacy: There are aspects of human nature and of the social order that generate moral sentiments.

A clearer argument against the view that religion enforces morality arises when we consider people who follow a rule in order to avoid threats and/or acquire pleasures. Can we be called moral if we avoid stealing only when a police officer is watching or contribute to charity only when we are applauded at a banquet? I think not.

The chief contribution that religion makes to morality is that it makes it easier for people to transform their lives. This is not an easy process and requires of people an act of faith that many persons cannot supply and few will sustain. A profound act of faith does not necessarily make us better; it only makes us more knowledgeable. We come to know God and through him to know ourselves. And what we learn about ourselves is, I suspect, quite unsettling. We are weak, greedy, impassioned, ill-tempered, and contradictory; we can barely be good any of the time, much less good most of the time. As Christopher Lasch put it, religion, far from putting doubts and anxieties to rest, tends to intensify them.[4]

The people for whom a religious experience heightens doubts and sharpens anxieties are people who are leading wasted or immoral lives. Religion does not solve their problems; it heightens them to the point that people finally feel they ought to do something about them. It creates an opportunity for personal transformation.

Consider the single most important organized example of personal transformation we have. It was created by neither churches nor businesses nor government, but by a few people whose lives had become unlivable. It is called Alcoholics Anonymous. Started in 1935, it does not impart a religion but uses faith in a supreme being as a motivation for transforming the lives of drunkards. We are not quite certain why it works so well. We have no data, in part because AA has no interest in generating data (and a good thing, too). But whatever makes it work for many (but far from all) of its members, it signifies the importance of self-discovery and personal transformation in human life.

Despite the general indifference of social science to religion, we can clutch at other bits of evidence. The Harvard economist, Richard Freeman, found that among black urban youth, other things being equal, those who were religious were less likely to be criminal than those who were irreligious.[5] Byron Johnson, a sociologist, has looked at the data and come to much the same conclusion.[6] There is even some sketchy evidence that faith-based prison programs are more likely to improve the lives of inmates after they are released than are rehabilitative programs that do not involve religion. And in every big city and many small cities in America, church-based groups are working at reducing delinquency, drug abuse, gang wars, teenage pregnancy, and single-parent homes. We have no systematic evidence as to whether these programs are working in any large sense—that is, for lots of people—but ample testimony that they do work in a small sense—that is, by changing the lives of identifiable individuals.

The evidence, though not conclusive, does suggest rather strongly that religion can make a difference in the lives of people about whom we worry—or ought to worry—the most. Can the government take advantage of the transforming power of religion without corrupting its use through heavy-handed regulations and endless litigation? To answer that question, we must acknowledge the great importance of the First Amendment to the Constitution and then deplore the sorry state of law that has emerged about its implications.

The second part of that amendment is the "free exercise" clause that denies the federal government the power to prohibit or require religious practices. It guarantees, in short, freedom of religious conscience. Not only does that rule keep the government's hands out of our religious—or irreligious—beliefs, it in addition facilitates the growth of religion by permitting new faiths and churches to spring up as people respond to them. There are some problems with enforcing the free exercise clause, in particular the problem of regulating behavior that may have a religious motivation. The courts have said we are free to believe but not necessarily free to act. Thus, the courts will not always allow what a religion commends. In consequence, it has allowed the government to ban Mormon polygamy and has not allowed the Amish to exempt themselves from paying Social Security taxes; it has upheld a ban on Indian use of peyote for religious reasons but has allowed religiously justified animal sacrifices.

Though the free exercise clause is a fount of continual litigation, its general purpose remains clear. It was well understood when first put into the Bill of Rights: No one, so far as anyone can tell, disagreed with the view that everyone should have religious freedom to worship or not as they saw fit. Nothing of the sort can be said about the preceding part of the amendment, the so-called establishment clause. No one, including whoever wrote it, has ever provided a clear understanding of it. James Madison proposed to the First Congress language that said that no "national religion" shall be established. Once it got to the floor of the House, it was changed to read "Congress shall make no law establishing religion." In the Senate, the language was still different: "Congress shall make no law establishing articles of faith, or mode of worship." Though different, all of these versions had two things in common: They were restrictions on what the federal government, not state governments, could do, and they were all aimed at preventing Congress from creating a church or telling people how to worship in one. What emerged from the conference committee was the ambiguous language we now have: "Congress shall make no law respecting an establishment of relig-ion."

What in the world does "respecting" mean? No one has any idea. The members of Congress who voted for it left no commentary, nor did anyone else. The Supreme Court, however, has created its own commentary. The decisive case was decided in 1947. In it, the Court allowed New Jersey to reimburse par-ents for bus fare to school, including to parochial schools. But before getting to this outcome, it announced that the "respecting" clause erected a "wall of sepa-ration" between church and state. That phrase was written by Thomas Jefferson in 1802 in a letter to a group of Baptists in Danbury, Connecticut. Jefferson, recall, was not at the Constitutional Convention and was not a member of the Congress that wrote the First Amendment. He was in no position at all to ex-plain what "respecting" meant. Moreover, he was a religious radical who had worked hard to separate church and state in ways that most politicians disliked. But the Supreme Court liked his phrase and decided that it is what the clause meant.[7]

Today it requires a lengthy textbook to describe the ways in which the Court has enforced the wall or permitted (as it did in the 1947 case) govern-ments to dig under, crawl over, or run around the so-called wall. Consider how often the wall is breached: "In God We Trust" is printed on our dollar bills and "One nation, under God" is part of the Pledge of Allegiance, but we cannot per-mit a Nativity scene to appear in a courthouse. The House and the Senate begin each meeting with a prayer and the government pays ministers of various faiths to be chaplains for the armed services, but we cannot allow a nonsectarian prayer to be used to begin a high school graduation. The federal government can use the G. I. Bill to pay the tuition costs of veterans attending religious as well as sectarian colleges, but states cannot supply financial aid to students attending parochial schools.

It is pointless to belabor the obvious: The Supreme Court has created case law about the establishment clause that is to some significant degree incoherent, but not uncodified. In 1972, the Court, in the case of *Lemon v. Kurtzman*, set forth three rules for deciding when a statute could involve religion. First, the statute must have a secular purpose; second, its primary effect must be one that neither advances nor inhibits religion; and third, it must not foster an excessive entanglement with religion.[8] But as Professor Henry Abraham has noted, on the very day that *Lemon* was announced, the Court decided that it was constitutional for the federal government to spend a quarter of a billion dollars for constructing buildings on private, including religious, colleges.[9] Among the reasons given by the author of this opinion, Chief Justice William Burger, was his claim that pa-rochial colleges are less involved in religious indoctrination than are parochial high schools. May I enter a mild dissent? I attended a relentlessly Baptist college where chapel was compulsory and I was given (as a Catholic student) a Baptist professor as my academic advisor who asked me why I did not become a Protes-tant.

The case law that has tumbled forward since the 1947 *Everson* decision cannot be reconciled by any set of rules. In 1947 New Jersey could reimburse parents for the bus fare they spent sending their children to parochial schools, but in 1972 the Court struck down an Ohio plan to give $90-per-year tuition rebates to children attending parochial school.[10] In 1980 the Court allowed New York to reimburse parochial schools for certain state-mandated expenses even though in 1977 it had overturned New York's effort to reimburse parochial schools for certain kinds of record keeping.[11] In 1992 the Court said that a rabbi could not give a nonsectarian invocation at a public school graduation but a year later allowed a student-led graduation prayer.[12] Pittsburgh can display a Hanukkah menorah and a Christmas tree on the steps of its city-county building but cannot put a Nativity scene inside its courthouse.[13]

The central problem that the Supreme Court has never faced is this: The First Amendment clearly prevents the government from requiring or imposing religious practices (such as a mandatory school prayer or paying tax money to a specific religious institution), but there is no substantial evidence that the framers of the First Amendment ever meant for it to ban nondiscriminatory government aid to all religions generally. The *Lemon* test is an error, because it forbids any government aid that might advance religion, no matter how nondiscriminatory the aid or the entanglement.

But there is another side to the problem of government aid to religious institutions. Federal money brings federal rules; and federal rules can harm, distort, or even crush religious experiences and greatly burden the small ministries of most churches and synagogues. Getting and accounting for government money is a task for a trained lawyer and accountant; most churches lack the services of such professionals. Though Congress might have the sense to modify the regulations now governing institutions it funds, left unchecked one can imagine a church membership being reshaped by equal employment criteria and church membership falling under the Americans with Disabilities Act. Government aid tends to turn aid recipients into the organizational equivalent of the bureaucracy that supplies the aid. The essence of the religious experience is, I think, not one that could be supplied under the aegis of the Federal Register and the United States Code. Imagine what would have happened to Alcoholics Anonymous if it had taken federal money. Its mission would have been shaped by government advisers and its appropriation defended by an AA pressure group.

I suspect many, probably most, Americans want to have the government—though not necessarily government aid—held at arm's length from religious institutions. Though there seems to be widespread support for allowing school prayer (a mistake, in my view), there is also widespread aversion to making religious activity mandatory. Americans are, more than the people of almost any other industrialized nation, religious; but as Professor Alan Wolfe has pointed out in his book, *One Nation, After All*, Americans are reluctant to impose religious views on other people. His data suggest to me that though Americans are opposed to a Constitutional wall of separation between church and state, they tend to support a cultural wall. That cultural wall seems to reflect the growing

American recognition of the fact that we are, indeed, a multicultural society in which every group owes every other one a substantial degree of respect. Wolfe suggests that Americans are loyal to "the essential truths of transcendental moral principles," but they are also willing to apply them flexibly.[14] By flexibly, Wolfe means with reasonable deference to the personal and cultural circumstances in which ordinary people find themselves.

If religion is an important source of possible personal transformation but any direct involvement between the government and religion will be denied by the Court, corrupted by Congress, and opposed by the public, what is to be done? I suggest that we must facilitate the movement of private funds into church-connected enterprises that have as their goal the kind of personal transformation that is required if we are to rescue people from social pathology.

A great deal of money—in 1993, as much as fifty-seven billion dollars— now goes from individual Americans to religious groups. Most of this money is to support churches and synagogues; not much, I suspect, is for important forms of religious outreach. And however the money is used, very little comes from corporations or foundations. Yet corporations contribute large amounts to secular establishments—schools, hospitals, and cultural entities.

We need a faith-based equivalent of the United Way. Not exactly the United Way, of course, but rather an independent organization that identifies useful faith-based outreach programs aimed at the kinds of personal misconduct— alcoholism, crime, delinquency, drug abuse, and single-mom pregnancies— about which Americans are so deeply, and so rightly, concerned. There are countless such church-based efforts. Professor John DiIulio and his associates have catalogued them in several cities. We now need to move beyond a catalogue and toward a switchboard that will direct private giving toward useful programs.

By "useful" a scholar usually means "empirically tested," but empirical tests are hard to arrange for small, understaffed, and underfunded activities. It would be better to limit the word "useful" to mean having passed a few simple tests: The program is aimed at reaching people at risk for harmful behavior, is financially honest and intellectually serious, and has won the esteem of knowledgeable observers. In time, perhaps we shall know more about such efforts; some might even be evaluated. But at the beginning, evaluation is much less important than effort.

The amount of money that could be raised by a United Way for Religious Outreach is not trivial. Corporations almost never give their charitable dollars to religious groups, in part because they believe, rightly, that supporting churches is a task for church members and in part because they fear, understandably, criticism from people skeptical of religious activity. But the employees of corporations can make contributions to a variety of enterprises in ways that lead to their donations being matched by corporate funds up to some annual limit. Rarely, however, are faith-based outreach programs on the list of charities approved for such matches. If in each large city there was a United Way for Religious Outreach, it could provide guidance for corporations willing to look for church-based outreach programs and for corporate employees eager to contribute to a particular kind of church outreach. Both corporations and individuals now give money to programs designed to help the needy, but only the largest ones attract support. The Salvation Army, for example, deservedly gets such support, but smaller versions of the same religious effort—small churches with one or two ministers and a handful of volunteers—get nothing.

Helping the kind of personal transformation that is the core function of religion requires that we expect no broad changes, little in the way of a mass movement, and not much in the form of verifiable data. Faith can only transform one person at a time, and then only as the result of the personal attention of one other person. This is not an activity of which research foundations or schools of public policy know much. Or care much. But it is, over the course of human history, a powerful force that has shaped nations and cultures. We ought not let Constitutional scruples or personal reservations impede what may be the last, best hope of the utterly disadvantaged.

Notes

1. Adam Smith, *The Wealth of Nations* (Oxford: Oxford University Press, 1976), 8.

2. David Hume, "Of Superstition and Enthusiasm," in *Essays: Moral, Political, and Literary,* ed. Eugene F. Miller (Indianapolis: Liberty Classics, 1987), 73-79.

3. Michael Oakeshott, *Religion, Politics and the Moral Life*, ed. Timothy Fuller (New Haven, Conn.: Yale University Press, 1993), 39-45.

4. Christopher Lasch, *The Revolt of the Elites and the Betrayal of Democracy* (New York: Norton, 1995), 16.

5. Richard B. Freeman, "Who Escapes? The Relation of Church-Going and Other Background Factors to the Socio-Economic Performance of Black Male Youths From Inner-City Poverty Tracts" Working Paper Number 1656 (Cambridge, Mass.: National Bureau of Economic Research, 1985).

6. David B. Larson and Byron R. Johnson, "Religion: The Forgotten Factor in Cutting Youth Crime and Saving At-Risk Urban Youth," www.manhattan-institute.org/html/jpr-98-2.htm (March 1999).

7. *Everson v. Board of Education of Ewing Township*, 330 U.S. 1 (1947).

8. *Lemon v. Kurtzman*, 403 U.S. 602 (1971).

9. Henry J. Abraham and Barbara A. Perry, *Freedom and the Court*, seventh ed. (New York: Oxford University Press, 1998), 288.

10. *Everson v. Board of Education*, 330 U.S. 1 (1947); *Essex v. Wolman*, 406 U.S. 808 (1972).

11. *Committee for Public Education and Religious Liberty v. Regan*, 444 U.S. 646 (1980); *New York v. Cathedral Academy*, 434 U.S. 125 (1977).

12. *Lee v. Weisman*, 505 U.S. 577 (1992); *Jones v. Clear Creek Independent School District*, 61 Law Week 3819 (1993), cert. denied by Supreme Court.

13. *Allegheny County v. Greater Pittsburgh ACLU*, 497 U.S. 573 (1989).

14. Alan Wolfe, *One Nation, After All* (New York: Viking, 1998), 300.

Part III

New Paradigm of
Faith-Based Programs

Chapter 6

Charitable Choice:
Promise of a New Paradigm

Stephen V. Monsma

When Congress passed the 1996 act restructuring the welfare system, it included a provision that at the time was ignored by the news media. Nevertheless, I suspect that in the long run this little-noted provision may prove to be as significant and as profound a public policy change as the entire rest of the act. I am referring to Section 104, the charitable choice provision, which asserts that when states allow for welfare services to be provided by private agencies, they must allow faith-based organizations to compete on an equal basis with secular providers for the opportunity to provide those services.

The story of charitable choice begins with a United States senator, a young Senate staffer, and a law school professor. The senator was John Ashcroft of Missouri, the staffer was Annie Billings of Ashcroft's staff, and the law professor was Carl Esbeck of the University of Missouri School of Law. In fact, the story begins even a little earlier than these three persons—in a consultation sponsored by the Center for Public Justice and Dr. Stanley Carlson-Thies. This consultation was held in the Georgetown Holiday Inn in order to consider faith-based nonprofit organizations and how they could be incorporated more fully into the public policy arena of the United States. Welfare reform was just starting to move through Congress and Carl Esbeck, who attended the consultation, went home and started thinking and reflecting on the events of the weekend. He thought: Why not put language together that would create opportunities for faith-based charities to be involved in the welfare program that was being debated in Congress. It so happened that one of his former students from the University of Missouri was Annie Billings who was working on Senator Ashcroft's staff. So Carl called up Annie one day and ran a few ideas by her and she said, "That sounds great. Why don't you put something down on paper." At that point Carl Esbeck wrote the language that provided the basic form for charitable choice legislation. He sent it off to Annie Billings. She gave it to Senator

Ashcroft who looked it over and said, "It sounds great to me," and proceeded to introduce it as an amendment on the floor of the Senate. After some modifications and compromises, it was adopted and is now Section 104 of the Welfare Reform Act of 1996. But why do I see charitable choice as holding the promise of a paradigm shift? In fact, I see it as incorporating not one but two paradigm shifts in how we think about and approach public policy.

The Role of Civil Society

First, it is a shift away from the old debate between liberals and conservatives over whether we need more government or less government. Since the 1930s much of the political debate in the United States has revolved around conservatives who, on the one hand, looked to the free market to provide prosperity and saw government involvement as a threat to a prosperous, healthy economy and society and, on the other hand, liberals who looked to government as a key ingredient to a prosperous, equitable society and saw the free market without a strong governmental presence as leading to a society with many problems continuing unchecked. For years conservatives and liberals, Republicans and Democrats, Reaganites and Ted Kennedyites, or in an earlier era, Taftites and Trumanites fought this battle with passion and sometimes with skill, each group convinced that its vision for America was right.

Today, however, there is an increasingly large body of thought that believes both sides in this long-standing struggle missed a third critically important element in the public policy mix. What both sides missed was civil society, that sector of society made up of a host of social structures standing between the individual on the one hand and the megastructures of big government on the other. Persons left, right, and center are beginning to see that shaping public policy solutions while ignoring voluntary associations, families, neighborhoods, religious congregations, and the host of other social structures within which most of us live our lives is the public policy equivalent of studying the Battle of Gettysburg while ignoring the physical terrain on which it was fought.

Thus, the new public policy paradigm for which I am calling and which I think charitable choice suggests is one that takes into account civil society. This initiative seeks to work with and through our civil society as it constructs public policy rather than simply ignoring it as irrelevant.

The Religious Nature of Civil Society

A second paradigm shift that charitable choice addresses—and this is one whose need I suggest is less frequently recognized in the United States today—involves recognizing that a majority of the private, civil society, health, and social service agencies have a religious background and nature. It does not assume that the religious dimension found in many civil society institutions is merely incidental to their primary nature.

Until very recently, at least, almost all journalists and scholars simply ignored the religious character of most of the socially active organizations of our civil society. I have read study after study of nonprofit agencies and their programs, their nature, their relationship with government—yet most never mention their religious character. Such studies seem to consider the religious character of these agencies as about as relevant to understanding them and their work as the color of paint on their buildings! John DiIulio once reported: "I didn't remember ever seeing anyone doing a standard regression on churches and crime. Every other factor—I mean everything you could imagine—had been studied. But no one had really looked at whether churches had any impact on crime in their immediate vicinity."[1] Religion was just assumed to be of no consequence.

The old paradigm also accepts the strictest concept of church-state separation which posits that government may not cooperate with or help support faith-based agencies or, if it does, may only cooperate with or support their secular aspects. Thus, the old paradigm assumes that secular and religious aspects of a faith-based agency can be neatly separated without doing any damage to the nature of an agency's program or its effectiveness. In short, the traditional public policy paradigm ignored religion and religious aspects of faith-based groups, leading either to their being excluded from programs of cooperation or to their having to downplay or tone down their religious emphasis. Religion, after all, was nonessential and expendable.

There are three problems with this old paradigm. First of all, it excludes some of the most effective programs, even some which may be the only programs of their kind in a given neighborhood. Teen Challenge and Victory Outreach, for example, have had success rates in dealing with drug addicts in the 70 percent range, while most secular programs have struggled to get out of single digits.

Second, even when faith-based programs are not completely excluded, their effectiveness is often greatly reduced. Joe Klein, in a *New Yorker* article, tells the story of Joy of Jesus, a Detroit job training program that dealt with the hardest to place among the unemployed.[2] In fact, the state of Michigan was so impressed with its success that it offered to fund it, but only on the condition that there be no more prayers or Bible studies as part of the program. The assumption was that you could split off the religious aspects of the program without doing harm to it. As a result, however, the program fell apart. The very thing that was at the heart of its effectiveness had been removed. Peter Berger, the sociologist from Boston University, touched on a basic truth when he posed the paradox that "the worldly contribution of religion is possible only if religion itself remains otherworldly."[3]

Third, the old paradigm discriminates against religion. Whenever government cooperates with and subsidizes all types of secular agencies, but refuses to do so in the case of religious agencies, it is pursuing an unfair, discriminatory policy that puts faith-based agencies at a disadvantage when compared with their secular counterparts.

Take two drug rehab programs across the street from each other. One is sponsored by the local AME Church—it is religious in its approach to the problem of drug addiction. Across the street is a secular agency. If the government would come and say, look, we will fund the secular agency, but the other is religious so therefore we cannot fund it, it would be pursuing a discriminatory policy. The members of the AME Church are paying taxes and participating in the society as are all other citizens, but their money would not come back to them in the form of supporting their drug addiction program while it would to the secular agency.

Thus, there needs to be a double paradigm shift that takes civil society into account, making a place for it at the public policy table and, in doing so, allowing the very large religious sector of civil society to participate fully without having to deny or tone down the very religious nature that often makes it so effective. This is why I find the charitable choice provision of the 1996 Welfare Reform Act, which restructures welfare services in the United States, so important. It is the first federal, nationwide attempt to incorporate successfully this double paradigm shift into an actual piece of legislation.

The actual provisions of charitable choice will illustrate why it is such a highly significant shift in public policy. In helping the needy, charitable choice has three key goals:

1. Utilization of the civil society sector, including its faith-based organizations.
2. Protection of the religious integrity of faith-based organizations.
3. Protection of the religious freedom of the needy.

Four basic provisions of charitable choice are:

1. If a state utilizes civil society-sector providers to deliver social services, it may not exclude faith-based providers.
   - This applies to state programs implemented under Temporary Assistance for Needy Families (TANF) and the food stamp, Medicaid, and SSI programs.
   - Government utilization of faith-based providers can take the form of purchase of service contracts or vouchers.
2. If a faith-based provider is selected, its religious identity and expression may not be censored or interfered with.
   - It may make employment decisions based on religious considerations.
   - It may not be required to take down religious art or symbols.
   - Its institutional autonomy is protected.
   - It may not be required to alter its form of governance or legal structure.
   - Audits may cover only the program receiving public funds as long as they are segregated from other funds of the faith-based organization.

3. A faith-based provider may not discriminate against a beneficiary because of his or her religion or refusal to take part in religious practices.
   - It may not refuse to provide services to beneficiaries based on religion.
   - If there is a purchase of service contract, no funds may go for worship, religious instruction, or proselytization.
   - If there are vouchers, this restriction does not apply.
4. If a beneficiary objects to receiving services from a faith-based provider, he or she has the right to obtain services from another provider.

Conclusion

Why is charitable choice so very important? First, it is based on the belief that civil society—including its faith-based organizations—has a vital role to play in meeting persistent social problems. It also recognizes that the religious character of faith-based organizations must be protected. It recognizes that their religious character defines who they are. Their religious character is essential to their success, not simply an afterthought of secondary importance. Second, charitable choice is important because its basic policy concept can be applied to many other programs. It can also be a model, a paradigm, to be followed in area after area. This is already taking place. In 1998, when Congress reauthorized the Community Service Block Grant Program, it made charitable choice applicable to procurement under this program. Senator Ashcroft later introduced a "Charitable Choice Expansion Act" that would apply the charitable choice model to many other public policy areas, and charitable choice bills have been introduced in several state legislatures.

The United States is a prosperous and successful country, but many today—including myself—are convinced that if our prosperity and success are to continue, our foundational civil society needs to be renewed and our public policies must strengthen, build upon, and make use of the structures of civil society, including its faith-based structures. This is what charitable choice seeks to do.

Notes

1. Joe Klein, "In God They Trust," *New Yorker* 73, no. 16 (16 June 1997): 43.
2. Klein, *New Yorker,* 48.
3. Peter L. Berger, "The Serendipity of Liberties," in *The Structure of Freedom: Correlations, Causes, and Cautions,* ed. Richard John Neuhaus (Grand Rapids, Mich.: Eerdmans, 1991), 16.

Chapter 7

Faith in Inner-City Youth: New Evidence of the Efficacy of Faith-Based Programs

John J. DiIulio Jr.

There is a trinity of obvious truths which connects faith to inner-city children. I say these truths are obvious even though I am a social scientist (a social scientist is one who engages in the elaborate demonstration of the obvious by methods which are obscure). I want to explain and advocate these three truths about the capacity, the extent, and the efficacy of faith-based approaches to the most severe social problems we have in America today. These are problems which, despite all the good news about crime, welfare, and all the other social indicators, we are far from having solved. In some respects we have not yet begun to address them.

The first truth is that America's most severely at-risk urban children and young adults—whether in South Central L.A. or in North Central Philadelphia, whether it is Boston or Austin—can and should be sheltered from violence, permitted to achieve literacy, to access jobs, and to reach adulthood in one physical, social, moral, and economically self-sufficient whole.

The second truth is that innovative partnerships among local organizations—public and private, for-profit and not-for-profit, religious and secular, big and small, suites and streets, and, if I can be afforded this alliteration, Gucci loafers and grass roots leaders—can come together and mobilize the human and financial resources that are necessary to resurrect hope and opportunity for our country's most truly disadvantaged urban children and young people.

The third truth is that, given such partnerships and given adequate financial support, faith-based youth and community outreach programs—whether we are talking about tall tower churches or about tiny blessing stations, whether we are talking about independent religious nonprofits or ecumenical coalitions or interfaith alliances—these partnerships, anchored in faith, can and will do more and

63

better if they are adequately supported. In fact, what they have always done in this country, from the very early days of the founding period to the present, to borrow Dr. Marvin Olasky's beautiful trilogy, is to provide a "personal, spiritual, and challenging" menu of social services from preschools to prison fellowships, from food banks to investment banks, devoting their volunteers, their buildings, their shoestring budgets, and yes, their prayers, to lifting up the poor, the oppressed, and the abandoned. They have been eager to deploy their spiritual capital to help leverage political capital, social capital, and financial capital in ways that positively transform—and transform positively—the lives of our worst-off urban children, young adults, and families.

I agree with my mentor, Professor James Q. Wilson, that social scientists sometimes have a bit too much love of quantification. But he also taught me that the plural of anecdote is not data. Still, let me begin with just a couple of anecdotes because I want to illustrate some things, and I promise I will inflict on you a little systematic data later.

In the last four and a half to five years I have been going around the country and looking intensively at dozens of small, faith-based organizations that serve inner-city communities. One example stands out most in my experience so far, and it was one of the earliest ones. That was the experience I had in Boston with the so-called Ten-Point Coalition led by the Reverend Eugene Rivers. I want to summarize very briefly what I witnessed there over a period of years.

Initially I witnessed record high rates of killing and youth violence in the poorest neighborhoods. About 85 percent of all violent youth crime in Boston was concentrated in just three neighborhoods of that area. Over a period of two and a half years, I heard the horrific noise of the nightly gunfire that Rev. Rivers' own children, Malcolm and Sojourner, went to bed hearing. He lives there in the neighborhood. But that noise has now ceased as the result of innovative partnerships among local police and probation officials and between them and the Dorchester-based outreach ministry of Rev. Rivers, Rev. Jeffrey Brown, Rev. Prince Woodbury, Rev. Harry Young, and others. I witnessed those partnerships succeed in effecting a twenty-nine-month period during which there was not a single gun-related youth homicide in the city of Boston. Since that period, there have been four. I will not say "only" four, because we have gotten too used to saying "only" in such matters. Four is four too many and we all know and feel that. But four is a lot better than the forty-four we might have had in this period were it not for these partnerships.

Among about two dozen things they were doing with their peripatetic pace, I witnessed just one of the programs of this ministry in the summer of 1998 where I watched them get up close and personal, individually, in the lives of some three-hundred kids. These youth had been identified by the Boston police and Boston school officials as having joined up with some pretty serious street gangs in Boston. They were sort of young thuggers and muggers in the making. Several of them had already been caught and adjudicated for a couple of violent crimes. I witnessed how, after intervening and getting up close and personal in the lives of these children, the kids were turned around. The word Professor

Wilson has used is exactly the right word—"transformed." I witnessed how these kids who at the start of the summer were solemn and angry and full of attitude, had begun to read and to write and to smile and to work and to otherwise turn themselves around under the awesome influence of unconditional love, delivered by responsible adults who lived where they lived, walked the streets where they walked, and were there for them for real, twenty-four hours a day, seven days a week, 365 days of the year.

Finally, I witnessed something even more amazing than that. I am a Philadelphia homeboy and we pride ourselves in Philadelphia on booing Santa Claus at Eagles games and throwing snowballs at the Easter bunny. We are a tough people, a tough crowd. We frankly do not believe much of what we hear about successes in other places, including New York. To hear all this good news about Boston in the *Philadelphia Inquirer* led a lot of my friends in law enforcement, including the district attorney of Philadelphia and our new police commissioner, John Timmoney, to think that this was a lot of hogwash. We did not buy it. Nevertheless we took twenty-four top Philadelphia probation, parole, and district attorney's people, as well as police, some of our clergy, and our department of recreation folks to Boston for two days. What they saw there so profoundly impressed them that they came back and over the past seven months have developed a Philadelphia version of this youth violence partnership that was so successful in Boston. While I will not say what the results have been, because it is too early to say, I will tell you that youth violence so far is down big time in the neighborhoods where this partnership has begun. This includes gun-related youth violence which, in Philadelphia, is the worst in the nation. (I am sad to say 82 percent of our homicides in Philadelphia are gun-related, the highest percentage in the country.)

I could go on with these kinds of anecdotes. But let me turn to the more systematic data and briefly discuss the efficacy of some of these programs.

In 1998 the Urban Institute, the grand think tank in Washington, D.C., published the results of a survey of faith-based service providers in the nation's capital. The survey found that 95 percent of the congregations in the district performed some kind of outreach service. Two hundred and twenty-six religious congregations provided a total of more than one-thousand community services to more than two-hundred fifty thousand individuals in the year 1996, according to that study. The services included food and clothing, financial assistance, and daycare. In fact, a third of all daycare in this country is provided directly or indirectly by religious organizations.

In the mid-1990s, there was a six-city survey of more than one hundred randomly selected churches and synagogues that were built in 1940 or earlier, which was an inventory of how these institutions served their communities. It was led by Professor Ram Cnaan, a wonderful professor of social work at the University of Pennsylvania. Professor Cnaan, by the way, describes himself as a "Jewish atheist." (A Jewish atheist is defined as someone who knows precisely what the God he does not believe in expects of him.) The study was commissioned by Partners for Sacred Places, an organization in Philadelphia dedicated to the care and good use of older religious properties. They wanted to know what was going on inside these important sacred places. The congregations were surveyed in Philadelphia, New York, Chicago, Indianapolis, Mobile, and the Bay Area of Oakland and San Francisco. Each church surveyed was subject to a rather extensive series of interviews. (He and I are now replicating, or actually doing a more fine-tuned version of this survey in Philadelphia, so we will have the definitive survey of this kind.) Ninety-three percent of the churches across these six cities opened their doors to the larger community. On average, each church provided more than fifty-three hundred hours per year of volunteer support to its community programs, the equivalent of over two and a half full-time volunteers stationed year round at each church. On average, each church provided about one-hundred forty thousand dollars a year in community programs, which was about sixteen times what they took in from the beneficiaries of these programs. So they gave sixteen times more than they received. Each church supported on average about four major programs and provided all sorts of informal and impromptu services as well.

But here is the truly important finding in that study and in numerous smaller studies that I could cite. Poor children who were not the sons and daughters of any church member were the primary beneficiaries of the programs of these churches in every single city. Unchurched children, people not otherwise affiliated with the church, benefited most from church-supported programs rather than the sons or daughters of churchgoers. This tells us something very important. It is not just about serving one's own congregation or one's own members. Many, many of these churches are pushing outside their own boundaries into communities that are different demographically from their own membership to make a difference.

There is a grand tradition of survey research on predominantly African American churches where these kinds of numbers and these kinds of results are very much similar to what Professor Cnaan found in his randomly selected, very scientific survey of church outreach in the United States. A 1990 study found that the majority of churches with urban addresses serving predominantly African American populations were providing all manner of social services.[2] Those data, interestingly, which reflected the 1970s and 1980s, sat there more or less unanalyzed or, at least, had to be reanalyzed. A reanalysis was conducted in 1997 by my colleague at Public/Private Ventures in Philadelphia, Rev. Dr. Harold Dean Trulear, who heads a program for religion and at-risk youth.[3]

Dr. Trulear found that African American churches not only were doing what churches in Professor Cnaan's study were doing, serving their communities and, in many cases, serving individuals who predominantly were not sons and daughters of church members, but they were the only sources of social service in these neighborhoods. If you compared them to child protective services, a formal governmental entity, they were handling roughly as many children who were in need of child protective services as the official agencies were.[4]

I could talk further about several larger studies. But let me share the results of one more study which is very near and dear to my heart. I had two Princeton students in 1996 who were the best students in my thirteen years at Princeton—Jeremy White and Mary de Marcellus. They wanted to see what happens when you get close to these churches and really go inside. Do they actually provide these kinds of services? The questionnaires and in-depth interviews are one thing. But what if we spend six months going into these neighborhoods and really getting to know these faith communities and what they are doing for children and at-risk youth and young adults? And how about if the professor were to fund that study? So I did, via Public/Private Ventures. And I could not be more proud of what they produced.

Basically, they went into Washington, D.C., mainly southeast Washington, D.C.—it is the poorest section of Washington, D.C., and predominantly African American—and they got up close and personal to 129 faith-based youth and community outreach ministries. Let me just briefly tell you what they found. This was a study of a relatively small population, but it was an intensive field-based effort at describing what these institutions do and how they operate. What Mary de Marcellus and Jeremy White found was that there is indeed a critical mass of faith-based organizations in Washington, D.C. that work directly and intensively with at-risk youth. Virtually all the children who are reached by these programs come from seriously impoverished families, most in neighborhoods that have high concentrations of violence or drug abuse. Excluding faith-based schools, in the faith-based programs that they surveyed and interviewed, they discovered that in total they worked with about thirty-five hundred youths in Washington, D.C. on a weekly basis.

Most of the ministries of these faith-based nonprofits or church-based groups were born of the vision and initiative of one individual. Almost without exception, each organization that they visited and profiled conjured up one name: Children of Mine—Hanna Hawkins, the Fishing School—Tom Lewis, the Children's Center—Myrtle Loury, Calvary Baptist—Paget Reed, the Unique Learning Center—Sherry Woods, and so on. Interviews they conducted suggested that the directors of faith-based organizations make enormous, seemingly irrational sacrifices to reflect God's unconditional love and their own love for these children. Few programs focused solely on evangelization. Instead, they focused on filling the daily practical needs and spiritual needs of the children by providing a safe haven, tutoring, and other productive activities.

As inspiring as that may be, such findings tell us only about the extent to which community-serving ministries are out there. Professor Cnaan says they are in place. Other survey research says the same. And good social science will continue to replicate these findings over and over again so that even a skeptical social scientist will believe what the smaller, more intensive field network studies say.

You could easily ask, "If they are out there, and they are out there in critical mass, and they are serving primarily children who are not members of their own congregations, why do we have such problems?" And that is a fair question. But ask yourself the other counter-factual question. What if they were not out there? How much worse would things be in South Central L.A. or North Central Philadelphia or downtown Detroit? How much more money would we need to mobilize? Where would the other volunteers come from? We know from the great survey work of George Gallup of the Gallup Institute, from an absolutely tremendous stock of data that he has gathered over the past fifteen to twenty years on the subject of the religious life of Americans, that the majority of volunteers and voluntary youth-serving organizations in this country come out of communities of faith. This is true in the toughest of circumstances serving the most at-risk populations as well. Without them, how much worse would things be? A lot worse. How much more would be needed to replace these efforts were they to disappear tomorrow morning? A tremendous amount.

What then about their efficacy? Is there any evidence for their effectiveness? Professor Wilson has discussed this. There is a body of social science evidence that begins to establish the proposition that, other things being equal, in the lives of our most severely at-risk children and young adults, especially those who are concentrated in inner-city neighborhoods like South Central L.A., religious influences tend to lead to better outcomes when we are talking about avoiding violence, achieving literacy, accessing jobs, escaping poverty, or virtually any socioeconomic outcome you can think of. Based on the data we have thus far, religious influences seem to be a pretty good bet. Professor Wilson referenced the study by economist Richard Freeman of Harvard University. That finding of Richard Freeman's was replicated recently in a reanalysis of those data and an updating by Dr. David Larson of the National Institute of Health Care Research in partnership with another researcher whom Professor Wilson mentioned, Byron Johnson, a criminologist at Vanderbilt University. They found, yet again, that if you want to explain the variance in the rates of young black male unemployment, or of who escapes poverty, or of who avoids trouble with the law, you better load up your regressions with some decent measure of religiosity or spirituality or churchgoing. That will explain a good deal of the variance. And those who are churchgoing, or have other religious influences in their lives, seem to do better over time, all things being equal.[5]

I would like now to address a question about Prison Fellowship Ministries. I have to be careful now because I am both analyst and advocate here. I joined the board of Prison Fellowship Ministries so you may take what I am about to say with a grain of salt. But let me reference a study in *Justice Quarterly*, by Dr. Larson, Professor Johnson, and two other co-authors who last year published a study looking at the impact of Prison Fellowship Ministries in New York state prisons.[6] They found that compared to otherwise comparable inmates who did not receive the intervention from Prison Fellowship, that was essentially Bible studies, those who received it recidivated (that is, were rearrested) one year out at the rate of 14 percent. Those who did not receive the intervention, but who were otherwise comparable, were rearrested at the rate of 42 percent. Now 14 percent versus 42 percent may not seem like an awful lot in normal everyday life, but in social science terms, it is a tidal wave. It is a huge difference. That study might be criticized, as any study, but I think it is a pretty good study. It is one of several that demonstrates the inverse relationship between churchgoing, religiosity, and other measures of spirituality and negative social outcomes—more religion, less crime; more religion, the greater your chances of escaping poverty. That oversimplifies, but it's the crux of what the latest and best studies conclude.

How do they do it? How does Teen Challenge, or Victory Fellowship, or Prison Fellowship Ministries, or small and medium-sized community-serving ministries do what they do? As Professor Wilson suggested, this is like trying to describe or catch lightning in a bottle.

Let me very briefly describe in the words of others what I think is going on. Robert Woodson is the president of the National Center for Neighborhood Enterprise and a three-decade veteran of trying to mobilize faith-based and secular grassroots activists in inner-city neighborhoods, lifting up, as he calls them, the inner-city "Josephs" who are out there fighting the good fight, trying to turn the at-risk kids into resilient kids. Robert Woodson [of the National Center of Neighborhood Enterprise] says, "I will never forget the sight of former felons and addicts washing pots and pans or scrubbing down pews in restitution for some violation of a program's rules. Previously not a threat of a death sentence or life imprisonment meant anything to these individuals who accepted homicides as a fact of life and anticipated a life span of under thirty years. Yet they had willingly accepted the discipline of an unpretentious sixty-year-old outreach minister because he had won their trust."[7]

But how did this minister, all 5'4'' of him, win the trust of these men? How do any outreach ministers win their trust and how do they sustain it? Dr. Eva Thorne recently received her doctorate in political science at MIT and is a young African American woman. For over a decade she has studied and worked side by side with Boston's Rev. Eugene Rivers. She explains: "It's spiritual, but in a way you can begin to break it down empirically." She continues, "The two fatal mistakes the so-called youth development experts, the professional therapists, all make are as follows: First, even if they do reach the most at-risk kids or young adults, which most don't, they reach them with programs, not people, with activities that never actually fill the moral and social void of positive, caring, one-on-one relationships. Second," she adds, "the mentoring programs that do put a responsible adult directly into the lives of high-risk kids and young adults nonetheless continue to relate to the youth as their clients, their beneficiaries, their problem child defined by the abuses the children suffered, the violence they have witnessed or done or had inflicted on them, the failures they had in school, the illicit acts they have committed, the illegal drugs they have consumed or sold, the low income neighborhood in which they have lived. Logically," she says, "you can't really expect much from a problem child." But what Dr. Eva Thorne calls the spiritual alternative is to understand and approach each child—each young person on probation, or, in the words of Rev. Rivers, "the older thugger and mugger, the crack head young girl who is one act away from becoming a crack head unmarried mother"—to approach each one not as a problem child, but as a child of God. God already knows all they have suffered and God alone knows how they have experienced the pain, the confusion, the anger, the evil. You become a spiritual presence, a together adult who, if asked, will tell them about the Lord and encourage going to church, but who, regardless, treats them as moral beings worthy of a mother's unconditional love, administered with a father's firm hand. And if they are hungry for the messenger, Rev. Rivers concludes, they are hungry for the new moral vocabulary, again, with or without religion per se.

In a rather similar vein, a young associate of Rev. Rivers, Rev. Jeffrey Brown of Boston's Union Baptist Church, compares an effective youth outreach ministry to what he calls "moral jujitsu." He describes what he means by this term. "A young life with so much negative forces coming at you," he says, "and in a sudden act of showing up, of being there in sincere and steadfast concern for their well-being, you use all that negative force against itself. You've pulled a child up off the mat. You are there with yourself, with your words and with your programs and activities to begin filling the void and to keep it filled with hope and with good possibilities. Hygiene changes, grades improve, gangs are no longer a desirable option. Soon the results literally speak for themselves."

That is about as close as I have gotten in four and a half to five years to statements from people who actually *do* rather than merely *study* this. It is as close as one comes to understanding what this transformation is about. But even the outreach ministers and volunteers will stress that the needy, the impoverished, the alone, the defeated, the hopeless, the inner-city youth we are mainly talking about here need spirituality provided in some broader context, what I have come to refer to as "Spirituality Plus." Based on everything I have learned from this systematic research, the ethnographic research, the soaking and poking, I would suggest that there is a way to know such outreach ministries when you see them. As the Supreme Court says about obscenity: "We know it when we see it." How do you know spirituality is at work when you see it? Spirituality is the foundation of seven lively virtues that are alive, I would submit to you, in effective youth outreach ministries.

Spirituality, the *faith* in faith-based, the *faith* in the faith factor, is what brings adult leaders and volunteers to their mission. If it is a school, it is a vocation, not just a job. It is not a nine to five life. It is not because you get the summers off. The people who work in these settings are the unbelievable saints who work at the little North Central Philadelphia school where I teach on a part-time basis. For them it is a mission, it is a vocation, even though they rarely proselytize or otherwise formally attempt to make converts. That is, if they are big E evangelicals, they lead, as Rev. Rivers says, by "putting their hips where their lips are."[8] They are evangelizing. "They are doing what Jesus wants us to do," he says. They say, "God bless you" even when people do not sneeze. They are unapologetic and love to get you into the pews if at all possible and, in some cases, get you saved. I know because many of my evangelical friends are trying to get me saved. I tell them that there is a little matter of excommunication that I need to consider before jumping aboard, for I consider myself a "born-again Catholic" and must leave it at that. But spirituality is the foundation. If you take the "faith" out of the "faith factor," what you have is social service delivery with a cross or other religious symbol perhaps, but no transformation will occur. "The name but not," as Rev. Rivers says, "the game." What are the seven lively virtues that you can build on top of this spiritual foundation? Let me just quickly enumerate them:

1. Morality—the ministers and religious volunteers lovingly but firmly articulate, enforce, and inspire adherence to a no-excuses, clear-cut code of good conduct in matters major and mundane. Take your hat off when you come into the vestry. My favorite sign, up in one of the church gyms, says "Absolutely no slam-dunking." And when a 4'5" kid looks at that sign and says, "I'll obey that," it builds self-esteem and teaches adherence to rules all at the same time.
2. Proximity—they understand because they are there in the neighborhood. It cannot be any simpler than that.
3. Availability—they are there in the neighborhood when and where the kids need them when crises erupt, as they do every day in these neighborhoods, not just nine to five. Let me quickly insert here that people who advocate faith-based approaches or want to explore them or push them the way I have been doing sometimes get into the habit of bashing social workers or bashing child protective services professionals. That is a very bad habit, I submit, because there are good people out there. The point, however, is that even the best of them cannot provide this personal, spiritual, challenging, and transforming way of approaching these children. They are prohibited from doing so by the administrative and other kinds of protocols under which they operate. Also, they take vacations, they get promoted, they go away. So even if they are doing everything they can do, the best of them cannot provide what these faith communities provide on the ground.
4. Safety—they provide an environment free of physical violence or threats as well as free of sexual predation.
5. Civility—they insist on and, in overt ways, induce courteous, respectful behavior.
6. Reciprocity—they require everyone to contribute. Everyone shares leadership burdens. Everyone does chores. Everyone serves others even as they are served. It could be something as simple as, "Yes, we're going to have this event, but you're going to set up the tables, and you're going to clean up afterwards." For many of these children, it's the first time in their lives that anyone has said to them, "I think you're worth being held accountable. You want something, you have to pay for it. You have to contribute. There is no free lunch. We love you, we're here for you, now set up the tables."
7. Last but not least, activity—these places are beehives of indoor/outdoor programs, discipleship activities, amusements, you name it.

Now one very important caveat with which I want to conclude. It is what I have come to call the doctrine named for my aforementioned Public/Private Ventures colleague, Rev. Dr. Dean Trulear. He was a youth outreach minister himself in Patterson, New Jersey, for many years. He was also dean of the faculty at New York Theological Seminary for many years although he has now been corrupted to work for an institution which is this big research intermediary. I noticed over the past year that he has hired four people, all of them people of overt faith. So the rest of the staff is a bit nervous. Having studied religion much more intensively than I have, and for a much longer period, and from the inside out, Trulear says, "When it comes to community outreach in the inner city, it is important to remember that not all churches, black or otherwise, are created equal. Naturally," he says, "it's in part a function of high resident membership. Inner-city churches with high resident membership cater more to high-risk neighborhood youth than churches which have inner-city addresses but whose members are increasingly and predominantly suburbanized or commuting congregations. The high resident membership churches," he goes on, "tend to cluster by size and evangelical orientation. It's the small and medium-sized churches, especially the so-called 'blessing stations' and specialized youth chapels with their charismatic leader and their small dedicated staff of volunteers that do a disproportionate amount of the outreach work with the worst-off inner-city youth. It's not the big churches, although some of them do a good job. It's the small and medium-sized churches, especially the ones where congregants and leaders live where the children do."[9]

So, when it comes to action against the plight of inner-city poor, when it comes to action against the problems of the children for whom we have the most to fear for their lives and for those around them, the reality is that churches cannot do it all, or cannot do it alone. And not all churches and religious faith-based nonprofits do it. But that reality should not obscure the enormous outreach tradition of the faith community that is alive and well in cities, as Professor Wilson suggested, all across the country.

I want to conclude by pointing you to someone in your own backyard. There is in South Central Los Angeles one of the most remarkable examples of a faith-based, church-anchored set of programs under the heading of the Los Angeles Metropolitan Churches. It is directed and led by Elder Eugene Williams.

I spent a very long day with Rev. Williams and I tell you, every time I do something like that, I am humbled. In 1999 Governor Wilson signed a new law that the Los Angeles Metropolitan Churches (LAMC) were instrumental in helping to get passed. It is a law that requires that GED and literacy training be conditions of an offender's probation for non-violent offenses. We are talking about a requirement for GED and literacy as a condition of probation for young adult felons. Governor Wilson recognized that the initiative put the church back into the middle of the community while allowing the church to be a major influence in solving problems that affect the community. Let me say as well that LAMC, like virtually all of the organizations I am talking about, neither asks for nor receives a penny of government money. To implement this initiative they did not go with their hand out and say, "If you can give us X dollars, then we will deliver Y services." They asked for a public authority to support and back up what the ministers and volunteers and network of churches wanted to do to service those men and women of their communities.

That is the model of an effective public/private/faith-based sector partnership. All play to their comparative advantage. But LAMC, like the hundreds of such entities around the country who are really doing the Lord's work in neighborhoods like South Central, requires human and financial support from surrounding private institutions, universities, and philanthropies. Professor Wilson suggested corporations and others. If community-serving ministries are going to reach critical mass and go to scale, as I think they can and should, we are going to need to support them. The rest of us, in sum, must support our urban brothers and sisters who follow Christ's call to love "the least of these." My favorite hymn—and be grateful that I will not sing it!—goes:

I, the Lord of sea and sky, I have heard my people cry:
All who dwell in dark and sin, my hand will save.
I, who made the stars of night, I will make their darkness bright.
Who will bear my light to them? Whom shall I send?
Here I am, Lord. Is it I, Lord?
I have heard you calling in the night.
I will go, Lord, if you lead me.
I will hold your people in my heart.[10]

Thank you, and God bless you.

Notes

1. Ram A. Cnaan, "Social and Community Involvement of Religious Congregations Housed in Historic Religious Properties: Findings from a Six-city Study," Final Report to Partners for Sacred Places, May 1998. www.ssw.upenn.edu/orsw/partners.doc (March 1999).

2. Eric C. Lincoln and Lawrence W. Mamiya, *The Black Church in the African-American Experience* (Durham, N.C.: Duke University Press, 1990).

3. Harold Dean Trulear and Tony Carnes, "A Study of the Social Service Dimension of Theological Education Certificate Programs: The 1997 Theological Certificate Program Survey," (New York: Ford Foundation, 1 November 1997), 34, 40-41.

4. Trulear and Carnes, Theological Survey.

5. David B. Larson and Byron R. Johnson, "Religion: The Forgotten Factor in Cutting Youth Crime and Saving At-Risk Urban Youth," www.manhattan-institute.org/html/jpr-98-2.htm (March 1999).

6. Byron R. Johnson, David B. Larson, and Timothy G. Pitts, "Religious Programming, Institutional Adjustment, and Recidivism Among Former Inmates in Prison Fellowship Programs," *Justice Quarterly* 14, no. 1 (1997): 145-66.

7. Robert L. Woodson Sr., *The Triumphs of Joseph; How Today's Community Healers Are Reviving Our Streets and Neighborhoods* (New York: Free Press, 1998), 93.

8. Interview with author, June 1998.

9. Trulear and Carnes, Theological Survey.

Chapter 8

Secularization of Faith-Based Organizations: Government Impact

Eloise Anderson

There is much discussion currently about charitable choice, which is an attempt to encourage more religious organizations to provide social services. My intent here is not to share a lot of data with you. Rather, since I started out in a faith-based organization, I want to share some of my observations about such organizations, as well as secular organizations, and what I perceive to be happening to them.

I have learned that my faith is very important to me and to a large extent directs my work. I also know that families, and many children, are at risk in this country. However, since only about 30 percent of households in the United States include children, when we think about social policy and interest groups pursuing the government for goodies, we should remember that most of the people pleading for goodies have no children. This is the first time that America has experienced such an increase in childlessness, and I am concerned about how that may affect our children. My belief is that the government is currently taking resources away from children and families and giving them to our past. We are paying for our past and not investing in our future. This suggests to me that we are not interested in our future as a nation.

I have been asked to address whether or not faith-based organizations and secular organizations are different. As we decide how to support faith-based organizations with tax dollars, there are several things we need to think about. My view is that over time faith-based organizations, if supported by tax dollars, will become secular in their approach.

When I sought information to accompany my observations, I asked such questions as: Who are they, these faith-based organizations? Most of them are located in the nonprofit sector. When one looks at information about the nonprofit sector, and then more specifically and narrowly at the charitable sector within that, there are some rather surprising but important realities to be faced.

To begin with, faith-based organizations in this country have been very strong since the late nineteenth and early twentieth centuries. Most of them, led by upper- and middle-class women who were locked out of the labor force, were established to address immigrants' issues. They wanted to effect change for the immigrants because they did not accept the immigrants as they were. They hoped, rather, to make them like themselves. That was my theory growing up and it has not really changed much except for who is doing it now.

If one looks at the histories of some of these organizations, one discovers discussion of the needs of the Irish or the Polish, never the English or the French, which is interesting. They wanted to change the immigrants not necessarily to Americanize them, but to make them middle class. Many of these programs were operated out of church organizations with the original intent of bringing a sense of religious and moral values to the Irish, the Polish, and other Eastern Europeans. They were concerned that they did not have the same sense of moral values. What I find interesting is that there were very few organizations, particularly in the North, that dealt with the migration of people from the South to the North. As a consequence, there were not the support systems around the southern poor who were migrating to northern urban areas—neither black nor white—that one finds for newly arriving Europeans. It is clear that there was a major difference between how we treated immigrants and how we reacted to southerners.

The second intent of these organizations, and I do not deny that it was a moral intent, was to relieve material distress. I like the words "material distress" much better than "poverty" because "poverty" suggests more than mere lack of material things. In this country there are very few of us, even the poor, who do not have material goods. I have been in a lot of homes which have a lot less money than I had, but who actually have more goodies than I had because they put their money into goodies versus things they need. There are, of course, reasons why they do this. As we look at what we want to do about the poor, we need to look at the notion of need, the absence of food or clothing or shelter.

Thus the charitable organizations of earlier days focused on the truly poor, but over time they have experienced huge shifts in their emphasis. If one looks at the census data and the IRS data (most available data comes out of the Internal Revenue Service, which is interesting), you see that charitable organizations are not what we might think. The majority are not social service organizations. They are hospitals (which I would not consider social services) and supporters of recreation, the arts, and other cultural affairs. We have a very few that are really dedicated to what I call social services. And among those are very few that provide direct material support. Some of them provide individual family services, with some providing day-care services. Many of them provide residential care (other than nursing homes), and some provide job training. And then there are some that organize for community involvement and advocacy.

As I began to look at this nonprofit sector, what blew me away was that there are about 1.2 million of these organizations throughout the country. And when I focused on an organization with which I am very familiar, the Catholic

Social Services, their data revealed something quite amazing. In 1997 Catholic charities had over nine million clients. If I add them to some other organizations that touch the lives of a lot of people, I would immediately expect that they touch the lives of the poor. But you can put that thought out your mind. Out of those 1.2 million organizations, very few actually provide social services. They seem to be everywhere, but in reality, there are relatively few of them. And only about seventy-five thousand of them actually deliver social services. What was shocking, since they have always been so visible, was that although these are large numbers, they do not comprise a larger proportion of the nonprofit world.

What is also interesting about these data is what is not there, particularly organizations that are tied to church congregations. Yet when we talk about faith-based organizations, we mostly think about organizations that are tied to a congregation. But we actually have very little information about them. In fact, I don't think we actually know who they are. And, what little we know only from observations may be very skewed. Programs that are auxiliary parts of churches or of the conventions and associations of churches are also omitted from the data.

So most of what we're talking about when we talk about faith-based organizations is what we see, not what sits in the data. That's perfectly all right, but I don't know whether or not we are prepared as a nation to do what we think we want to do with charitable choice, given what we don't know.

The annual reported revenue of nonprofit organizations amounts to about fifty-five billion dollars. These are not poor organizations. The ones that have the most money are, of course, the larger organizations. Where their funds come from surely is an important key to how we may expect them to perform over time. As a matter of fact, they receive very little of their money from cash and in-kind donations. (In-kind donations can include the time and energies of volunteers which is technically considered an in-kind donation. But the volunteer element is very small within these organizations.) To be sure, many of them receive a lot of their funds from the United Way, from community giving. Some of them get funds from their religious affiliation. But the big provider of funds is government—state, local, and federal.

This is a shift from what existed in the late 1950s and 1960s. In fact, it represents a massive shift of how they are being funded. Foundations fund some but not as much as they previously funded when I worked in a community organization.

And who do they serve? We have this notion that they serve poor people. But throw that away. Only 27 percent of these agencies serve the poor as the majority of their clients. Twenty percent of the organizations serve people who are "somewhat poor" (20-50 percent of their client population). Fifty-three percent of these organizations serve a clientele of which less than 20 percent are poor. And more significantly, only 16 percent of these organizations provide material assistance, food, clothing, and housing, usually called homeless shelters. So, this is not about serving the poor. It is totally different than what I would have expected, but it does seem to be consistent with my observations.

So what kind of organizations are actually serving the poor? As a matter of fact, employment and training agencies are the ones mainly serving the poor and very few of them are faith-based or connected to religious organizations. So as we move toward promoting faith-based involvement, these are some of the things we need to consider in developing policy.

When and why did this shift occur and how did it occur? My investigations indicate that a couple of key things happened. The first was in the 1930s with the Social Security Act. I don't believe that people yet understand the full impact of the Social Security Act. What we tend to look at is welfare, meaning the money we actually give to poor families, and its impact on social service agencies and the community development aspect. But when the federal government began to take over human services and social programs, we began to see a gradual shift in faith-based organizations.

The second big change occurred in the 1960s with the Great Society. At that time there was another significant change in faith-based organizations as the government began to develop community organizations. Thus, in many communities you will find faith-based organizations such as the Catholic Social Services, the Lutheran Social Services, and the Jewish Social Services, but beside them, at the same time, more private nonprofit organizations that are similarly situated, doing similar things, but funded totally by the government without the underpinnings of religious support. Thus, the government was developing organizations as well as church organizations within poor communities.

Until the 1960s half of our organizations were still being managed under the umbrella of faith, while secular organizations were very different. But by the 1980s there was a complete shift. Faith-based organizations had become extremely secular while secular organizations stayed secular.

Then, during the 1980s President Reagan set us on a different course. He devolved resources away from the central control of federal agencies back to local governments, raising the possibility for genuine change.

In addition to these major historic influences on faith-based organizations, there is yet another development. That has been what I call the credentialism of the human service worker, the need to become "professional" (excuse me, but I hope academics will take this gently). I call this the license to operate. And here I want to give you a story.

When I decided I wanted to go into sociology and described to my mother what I wanted to do, she said, "Any good person with common sense can do that. Why do you need the degree? Family counseling is the same thing. You know, this is what you got from your grandmother. Why do you need to have a degree in all this stuff?" So my family was quite confused by anyone wanting to spend four years in college to have a degree in something where they were not going to make anything or do anything except faithfully pursue what they ought to be doing for their own family.

The professionalization of charitable work had another impact on what happened to faith-based organizations and the development of more secular organizations. With this new development in the schools of sociology and the schools of social work, we began to see a subtle move away from an emphasis on mitigating material deprivation (poverty), as economic dependence, to a broader view of enhancing human development. And that says something about what we think we can do to humans and reflects what the schools of social work try to do. They dropped the notion of reducing poverty and economic dependency and began training to do something other than what they originally said they were about.

These two major influences, government funding and the professionalization of social workers, changed the behavior of faith-based organizations.

So where are we today? I think we had dreams of long ago and far away. That's what I like to call it. I read about all these people who are leading us through welfare reform, to go back and do what we did in the nineteenth century, how we ought to bring faith-based organizations back on the scene. But have these people ever really worked in a faith-based organization? Do they really know what's happening here? In my view, we can't recapture those days because we are not the same people.

There may be a way that we can pull faith into our work in a very different and meaningful way. But we have a view of religious affiliation that is based much more on myths about what we think we see in the world than on reality. As we look at the data, we discover things may not necessarily have been the way we thought they were when these organizations based on faith worked with the poor. I tend to think that many of these organizations worked with the poor in former days because many women were very bored and needed something gratifying to do. It was not poor women out there doing the work. They did not have people to come and take care of their families. If you look at who the women were who were driving those systems of social services, what you discover are class issues. Professionalism arose because of women's need to become competent outside the home. The search for professionalism was driving a lot of what was going on under the radar screen as it relates to the poor and to organizations that deal with the family. We need to be very cautious about what I call the technological freedom of women. We have not dealt with their displacement from the home as well as we did for men in their displacement from the home.

The second thing, which I think is driving us to emphasize faith-based effort, is a desire to have organizations that are "in the community." I have never figured out what this "community" is that we want the organizations to be in. Many say they want to be in poor communities, but we very seldom have these organizations in rural communities that are often the poorest communities of all. They are usually in urban areas. And the discussion about urban areas, it seems to me is usually a discussion about people of color. So when we ask, "In whose community?," it seems to me that we forget that the people who are going to service these communities, even though they might look like people there, do not always live in those communities. We have the notion that because I look like you, I am you, and that's not true. White ethnics are my best example of how diverse an ethnic group can be. So as we develop an organization because it will be closer to the community, I think we fool ourselves about what it is we really want to do.

A third thing, which probably concerns me more than most, is the notion that a faith-based organization that is doing good work, and Professor Fagan mentions this, can be duplicated and expanded. If you look at the behavior of older, more established affiliated organizations like the Catholic Social Services, the Lutheran Social Services, and Jewish Services, and then look at their secular counterparts, there is no difference.

Several things seemed to have happened. Most of my work has actually been done in organizational development because I don't think you can get the policy changed unless you do the organizational work. But when I look at the organizational structures of these organizations and consider how they have changed over time, I see several developments. One is niche development. Those of you who deal with that kind of theory, particularly those of you in business, clearly understand what I mean by niche development. There are social service agencies all working together in the same little niche so they only compete with one another. However, they usually have their geographic areas in which they serve and if you go into communities and find where they are, they're usually not housed close to each other. If they are, they do not work with each other. So they each have their own geographic territory that they have arranged and they feel pretty safe in that.

But, then, as they begin to rely on government support, their environment inevitably changes them. Now government regulators decide how they ought to operate, so they must conform to the regulators' dictates. And, if you look inside the government to see who runs government agencies and guidelines, they are not believers in faith-based programming. They design how the programs are going to look and how the organizations that receive "their" money are going to operate. The first thing you get when your faith-based organization begins to take government funding is a demand that your organization move in a direction inconsistent with its faith-based teaching.

Furthermore, once the regulators decide how things ought to look, the governing body of the organization then begins to change because of the government's demands about who ought to be on your governing body and what they ought to look like. Usually your governing body, the board of directors or trustees who steer the organization, move from being faith-oriented people to being more diverse. Though they are directors and trustees serving on the boards of faith-based organizations, they begin to change fundamentally and philosophically.

Another thing that happens, because organizations are like humans and because they are run by humans, is that as they work together they take on normative issues, which means they want the value sets of their peers. They become like their peers. And if their peers are secular, then they become more secular. So you find the organization becomes much more secular than it had been earlier because of the new niche in which it exists.

The third thing that happens is what I call the cognitive piece. This is the internal workings of the organization—who is hired, who is the staff, who is the leadership. They become the "professionals" who have the licenses to operate. They bring secular thinking and views into the organization because they got their licenses to operate from secular organizations.

As these three things lead faith-based organizations to become secular, most people are not aware of what is happening. It is like the frog in the hot water. If you drop the frog in hot water, he'll jump out; but if you slowly turn the heat up, he'll wind up being scalded to death before he knows what has happened. This is exactly what I think can happen to faith-based organizations. Everything, I believe, wants to adapt and to maintain itself. So you now have organizations that were faith-based but which are moving more toward being secular in order to adapt and to survive in their environment.

Finally, we create a management team to provide organizational leadership and encourage them to become "strategic." We even send them to school to learn how to do this. We teach them to think "strategically," to move further and further away from their faith-oriented mission, to position the organization to survive and grow. They marshal the organization's energies internally and externally for survival and growth, focusing their attention on their marketplace. This is not what their vision and mission originally were about. But if they are going to survive, these are the kinds of things they feel they have to do.

Most management in these organizations has been extremely effective. So to carry out their strategy, they do two things by way of managerial tactics. First, they become very efficient inside the organization. They are able to produce services with a lot less financial resources than other organizations, which is one of the reasons we are now interested in giving work to faith-based organizations. We believe that they are going to be more efficient than others.

The second tactic is to become politically shrewd. Since I have dealt with them both internally and externally, being one of those political operators and then having them operate on me, I've learned several things. To resist the regulators, they decouple themselves, they conceal, they buffer, they challenge, they attack, and they manipulate. And they do all this to survive. This is no different than secular organizations. They are now totally secularized.

Most small congregations, the ones that we think we want to give tax dollars to for all the reasons we stated earlier, should have a couple of clauses about what is required of them. One is that the community in which you want them to serve must be the community they know. We must get away from the notion that if you look like someone you therefore are like them. We have to understand that people of color who live in urban areas are just as ethnic as Europeans. Middle-class people, no matter who they are, have difficulty dealing with lower class (by income) whether they are middle-class whites or middle-class blacks. There is no difference. Once we understand that, we can better understand where we should put our tax dollars. We will find, for example, that many big churches in the inner city that can handle such programs have a membership that is often not from the inner city.

Same color → not the same people
DISAGREE!

The other thing we should understand about small faith-based organizations is that as we give them more and more public funding, we may move them away from their fundamental principles because we haven't changed the notion that government should not be involved with faith issues. The people who staff the various governmental organizations still have this view. Their staff members write guidelines for proposals they will accept based on what they believe. So we are not going to be able to have a faith-based organization stand true to its principles given how funding occurs because we have not changed the government gatekeepers.

The last questions we come to, since policymakers in the United States often make policy based on anecdotes and personal stories that are not necessarily the whole picture, are related to effectiveness, replication, and expansion. Why are some programs more effective than others? Are faith-based organizations that really work simply being led by charismatic personalities? As we consider their success, is it the program design of the organization that is working or is it a charismatic personality that makes it work? We don't know the answer to that.

Then there is the question of replication. Can we take this program and replicate it in other places? We don't have the answer for that yet either.

Finally, can I expand it without collapsing it? We have no answers to that either.

As we attempt to expand the role of our faith-based organizations, we need to answer these questions. Will these very successful programs, what I might call "mom and pop" organizations, be able to develop with assistance from government funds? My theory is that they will become secular in their behavior the way their predecessors have. They will do what all organizations do, to position themselves for life.

[handwritten margin note: what is the focus of the success of faith-based programs?]

[handwritten note at bottom: Faith based programs will become secular after receiving government aid in order to fit in and continue to receive this aid.]

Part IV

Public Policy and the Family

Chapter 9

Family and Religion: The Center Beam and Foundation of a Stable Nation

Patrick Fagan

It is a real honor to be here. I am realizing how impressive what Pepperdine is doing in this annual conference on Faith and Public Policy is becoming. It is vital and critical and they are doing it exactly right. I certainly hope that it will grow and blossom because the nation needs what is being done here. The Supreme Court will be confronted with decision after decision over the next twenty to thirty years because issues related to faith and public policy are coming more and more into focus as our nation decides whether we will pursue the ideas of the founders, based on faith, or choose another direction and essentially not be the same United States anymore. Pepperdine has carved out a niche that will be valuable to the public policy debate. It is going to grow.

My policy work has been to illustrate, from the data of social science research, what our ancestors—our grandparents and our great-grandparents—all knew. They never debated it, and if they were here this morning, they would say, "You have to do all that work to come up with that result?" Bill Bennett had a great phrase for much of the social sciences: "They prove the obvious by means that are obscure and very expensive." Nevertheless, let's look at the data which are the stuff of the social sciences.

Figure 9.1. illustrates what is happening to the children who are born in this country, whether they are born within or outside marriage. You can see that the out-of-wedlock birth cohort of the last couple of years has grown from a very small number back in the 1940s. In most nations, human frailty has always led to some out-of-wedlock births and always will. But a society that is successful is able to contain it fairly well. In the 1940s it was down around 3 percent. Now it has grown to 33 percent. By the way, there is some good and bad news about this 33 percent. The reason it has leveled off is that our teenagers are becoming increasingly chaste, while the twenty- and thirty-year-old's are continuing to give birth out of wedlock in growing numbers.

When we combine the two, we have a flat line. The data reveal that there is a real change taking place across the nation, and the good news is coming overwhelmingly from our younger generation.

Figure 9.1. Married and Out-of-Wedlock Births
Source: NCHS Vital Statistics[1]

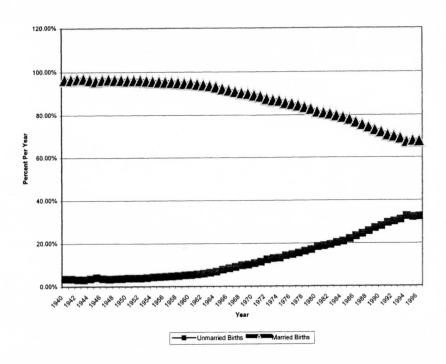

Next, in Figure 9.2., one can see the relationship between how close girls are to their fathers and whether or not they remain virgins. Note that all individuals in these data are unmarried, both virgins and non-virgins. On the extreme left is the group that is not at all close to their fathers. As you move across the chart, they are coming closer and closer to their fathers. When you focus on the group of girls who are very close to their fathers, you can see the massive impact that closeness has on their capacity to preserve their virginity. I am going to return often to this issue of virginity because it is the flip side of marriage, which is another key goal of the good society.

By the way, God accepts every child that comes from every father whether married or not. They are all made in his image, and he loves them all. However, as this chart shows, whether or not their earthly fathers love them all is the big question with big consequences.

Figure 9.2. Teen Feels Dad Cares: Virginity Rates

Source: NLS Ad Health; Robert Lerner Ph.D., The Heritage Foundation[2]

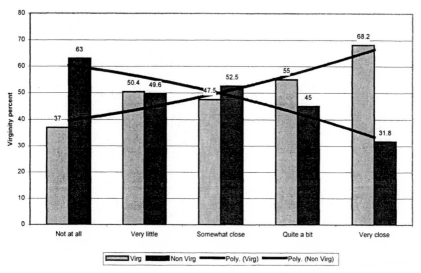

In Figure 9.3. are the two groups. If you look nationally at where the out-of-wedlock births are happening, you can see it is three times greater for those whose parents are not living together or are not married. The out-of-wedlock birth rate is overwhelmingly a result of the broken family. It is the second iteration of the broken family. I suspect that these girls were not probably that close to their fathers, though the mere fact of being married does not make fathers perfect, as we all know.

Figure 9.3. Percent Who Had Out-of-Wedlock Birth Later: With Whom They Lived at Age Fourteen

Source: NLSY 95[3]

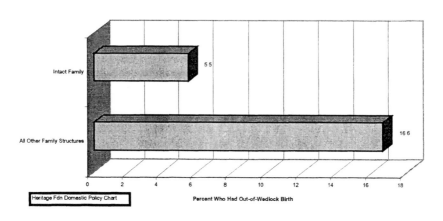

Figure 9.4. is the number of children in the United States who each year experience the divorce of their parents. In 1950 it was about a quarter of a million children per year. It peaked in the late 1970s and early 1980s, and since then has been fairly level at just a little over one million children a year.

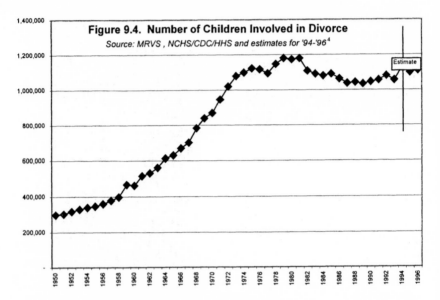

If we look at all American children who are under the age of eighteen (Figure 9.5.) and ask where they live and with whom they live, we find that 47 percent are living with parents who are in their first marriage. Twenty percent are in step-families. Six percent live with cohabiting parents. Thirteen percent are with a divorced single parent and one percent are with a widowed parent. It is worthy of note that this chart depicts all children under age eighteen, including one-year-olds and two-year-olds. But if we look at American children at age eighteen, not just all children under eighteen, we find, only 40 percent of American children reach the beginning of adulthood with their mother and father living together with them.

If we look at what has happened to us as a nation, we find that in 1950, for every one hundred children born, twelve entered a broken family. There are two entry points to a broken family. You can be born out of wedlock or your parents can divorce. Figure 9.6. graphs the ratios of those born out of wedlock and those experiencing their parents' divorce. In 1950, for every one hundred children born, twelve children entered a broken family. By 1993 this had risen to fifty-eight and last year, for every one hundred children born in the United States, sixty children entered a broken family. That is what is happening to our children. Which means that in the United States the vast majority of American mothers and fathers cannot stand each other enough to stay together to raise the child they brought into existence. This is not a situation that we are heading into.

For quite some time now, we have been a nation of deep alienation between the sexes. It is one of our major cultural characteristics and we must find a way to heal that.

Figure 9.5. Where the Children Are by Family Structure

Source: Consumer Finance Survey 1995, Federal Reserve Board[5]

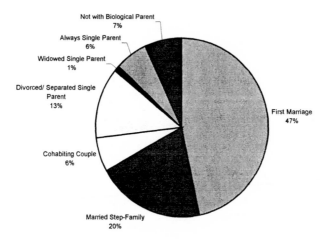

Figure 9.6. Children Entering Broken Families as a Proportion of Children Born

Source Unknown[6]

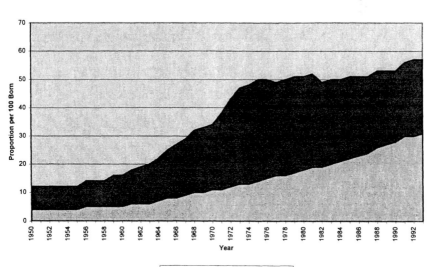

Last year, as noted earlier, for every one hundred born, sixty entered into a broken family leaving 40 percent living with mom and dad. Comparing different ethnic groups, some major differences emerge. Among white-Caucasians that figure is roughly at 50 percent (Figure 9.7.). Hispanics experience pretty much the same (Figure 9.8.). For African Americans only about 27 percent are living with their mother and father (Figure 9.9.). The strongest ethnic group for family life is the Asian American family where about 75 percent live in intact families (Figure 9.10.). I think that has a huge impact on why they do so well in college. They have a stable family life with parents who are committed to each other. So all of us have a lot to learn from our Asian American fellow citizens. Once I saw this data about Asian families, I saw Asian American mothers and fathers very differently.

Figure 9.7. White Children Eighteen and under by Family Structure
Source: Survey of Consumer Finance 1995 (See note 5)

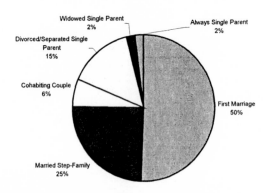

Figure 9.8. Hispanic Children Eighteen and under by Family Structure
Source Survey of Consumer Finance 1995 (See note 5)

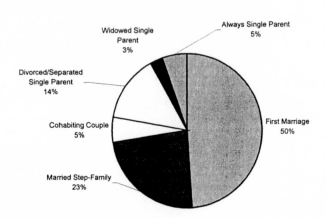

Figure 9.10. Other (Mainly Asian) Children Fourteen to Eighteen by Family Structure

Source Survey of Consumer Finance 1995 (See note 5)

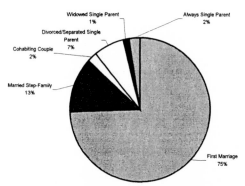

Next is the data on abortions in the United States. Figure 9.11. traces the total number of abortions broken into two categories: those that took place among married mothers and those that took place outside marriage. Abortion is not confined to the unmarried, but overwhelmingly it is outside marriage. This is a very

Figure 9.11. Estimated Surgical Abortions Within and Outside Of Marriage

Source: Alan Guttmacher Institute Data and Research[7]

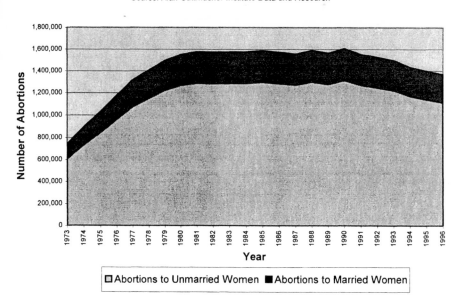

steady pattern. The Alan Guttmacher Institute, Planned Parenthood's Research Institute, which is very careful in its research, did two national surveys, the most recent one about three years ago. Their data points are exactly the same to the decimal point across all the categories. I was amazed at this because normally you will find fluctuations between surveys, but the results were exactly the same.

When one considers family structure and family income, it is obvious that wealth and marriage are highly related. As you ladies remember (unless you were so blown over by all his good looks, his great sense of humor, his fantastic kindness, and the shining knight in armor that he was), you or certainly your parents were eager to know how good a provider he was going to be. Potential income is one of the key considerations in getting married.

Using federal survey data, which is the data used throughout most of this analysis, the intact family has the highest income (Figure 9.12.). The average married family's median income is forty-eight thousand dollars. The step-family income is slightly lower, between forty-five thousand and forty-six thousand dollars. Then there is a big drop to the cohabiting couples' income and to the divorced or separated family. Finally, the single-parent family is at the bottom.

Figure 9.12. Median Income by Family Structure:
Families with Children (Without Transferred Income)
Source 1995 Survey of Consumer Finance
Kirk Johnson Ph.D., The Heritage Foundation [8]

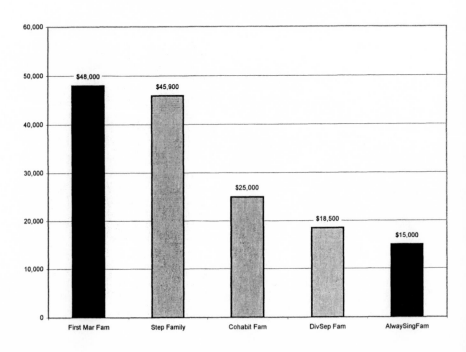

If we look at couples between the ages of fifty and sixty, we see that they have accumulated on average about one-hundred thirty thousand dollars worth of wealth (Figure 9.13.), most of it wrapped up in the family home. That category is a combination of two types of married families: step-families and the always marrieds. Next, the divorced group, is down around thirty-thousand dollars. And every other family category is lower than that. The stability of marriage has a huge effect on the accumulation of wealth and income over time.

Figure 9.13. Median Household Wealth by Marital Status (Ages 51-61)

Source: J.P. S.mith, RAND 1994, Marriage and Asset Savings [9]

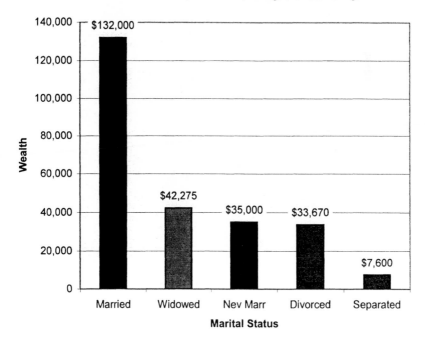

The average and median drop in income for divorced families with children is also quite dramatic (Figure 9.14.). Before the average divorce, the child is in a family with about forty-three thousand dollars of wealth. But it drops down to twenty-five thousand dollars, on average, after divorce. That is a much bigger drop for the family than the Great Depression ever caused. Divorce visits on families such a massive blow to their whole income and capital that it dwarfs the Great Depression. Over a million children go through that experience every year. More people drop below the poverty line because of divorce than for any other cause, including out-of-wedlock births.

Figure 9.14. Impact of Divorce on Income of Families with Children

Source: Corcoran & Chaudray unpublished research paper. Survey Research Center, University of Michigan, Ann Arbor, May 1994 [10]

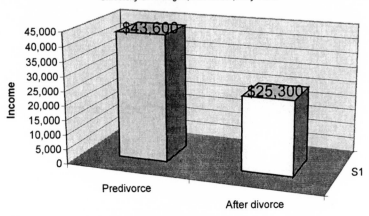

Figure 9.15. traces the rates of poverty. The lowest is the rate of family poverty among married families. Childhood poverty is a favorite issue in the media, but you probably will not see the data from this perspective. In first marriages, 10 percent of children in intact families are in poverty. Slightly less, 9 percent, of step-families are in poverty. (By the time the step-family is formed, couples

Figure 9.15. Percent of Child-Raising Families in Poverty by Family Structure Type

Source 1995 Survey of Consumer Finance
Kirk Johnson Ph.D, The Heritage Foundation [11]

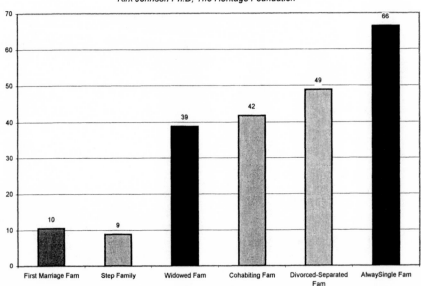

are normally a bit older, a bit further along in their career track, and incomes are just a bit higher.) Poverty among widowed families is much higher, at about 39 percent. Next is the cohabiting mother and father at 42 percent, and 49 percent for the divorced single parent. (Normally it is a single mother, since after divorce children normally stay with their mother.) Finally, with the always-single mother, 66 percent are in poverty. The single biggest issue in poverty is marriage.

For the serious abuse of children, we switch to British data (there are no U.S. data—you can't find them). These data are a dagger in the heart of the feminist critique of the patriarchal family. Notice where the serious abuse of children takes place. The lowest incidence of child abuse is in the intact married family, where the biological mother and father are together. The intact family is the safest place for a child. Abuse is six times higher in the step-family. Where the mother is living alone with the child, the likelihood of serious abuse is fourteen times higher (Figure 9.16.). Where the father is living alone with the child, it is twenty times higher. Where the biological parents are cohabiting, the real mother and the real father, not married, but only cohabiting, it is twenty times higher as well. And the most dangerous place for the child is when the mother is cohabiting with a boyfriend, where serious child abuse is thirty-three times higher.

If you consider the abuse of children who die—fatal child abuse—the likelihood in this last category is seventy-three times higher. In the future, because these cases often hit the front pages, watch and read carefully, and you will discover that the vast majority of cases of such abuse involve the mother cohabiting with a boyfriend.

Figure 9.16. Risk Rates of Serious Abuse to the Child

Source: Family Education Trust UK[12]

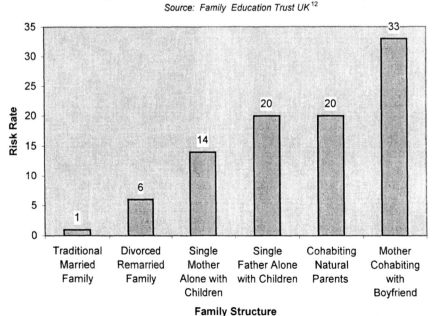

Although I could find no data on the rate of abuse for grown women by family structure, I suspect that it would be much the same. Other research indicates that where the child is abused, the mother also tends to be abused. The feminists, of course, studiously avoid this body of data.

When we search for relationships between juvenile crime and family structure, the state of Wisconsin is the only state that has collected relevant data. If we ask where juvenile crime takes place, data on incarcerated juvenile criminals are probably going to be biased a bit in favor of intact families because they tend to have the money to hire the lawyers to get their kids out, while the poorer do not. With that caveat, Figure 9.17. shows that for every child who is incarcerated from a two-parent family (both step-families and always-intact families), there are four from families where parents are married but separated. There are twelve from divorced single-parent families and twenty-two from always-single parents.

Juvenile crime is massively connected with family structure. If you want to reduce crime, you increase strong marriages. If you want to reduce poverty, you increase intact marriages. If you want to reduce child abuse, you increase marriage.

Figure 9.17. Juvenile Incarceration Ratios in Wisconsin by Family Structure 1993

Source: Wiscosin Dept HSS and CPS 1993[13]

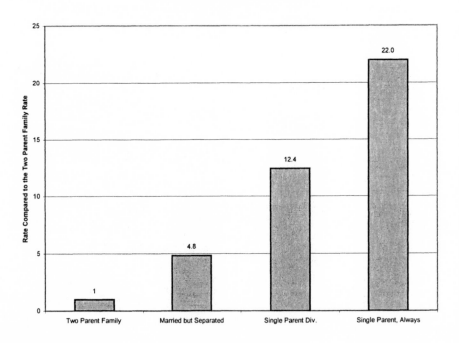

If we are truly serious about the quality of life in our nation, we will ultimately need to consider issues of faith and worship. Figure 9.18. shows national income data for 1993 for four groups—broken and intact families who never went to church and broken and intact families where the children were weekly churchgoers. The average income of these children when they reach their thirties shows that the lowest income is among children from the broken family that never went to church. Next lowest is the intact family that never went to church. The next higher one is the broken family that went to church each week. And finally, the highest of all is the intact family that went to church every week. In a piece of research done in 1986 by a Harvard professor (Richard Freeman) tracing which children escaped the grinding poverty of the inner city, the leading indicator was that they came from families that went to church each week. That piece of research, done fourteen years ago, has yet to be replicated. According to this research in the massive debate on poverty, the leading indicator of who will make it out of poverty ends up being kids who grew up in families that worship God every week.

Figure 9.18. Family/Church Background in 1979 and 1982; Income in 1993

Source: NLSY 1993 [14]

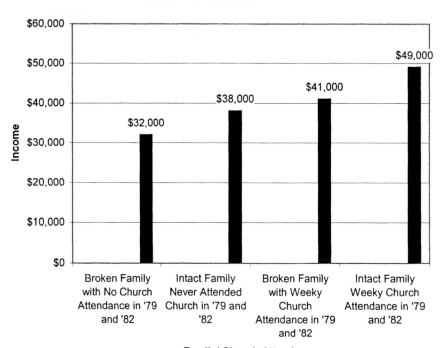

Family/ Church Attendance

Given the devastating effect of teenage and out-of-wedlock pregnancies, the data related to the impact of the parents' worship on children's virginity is significant (Figure 9.19.). It turns out that among teenagers between ages thirteen and seventeen, if mother and father do not worship, 61 percent of their children are still virgins. If the mother-only worships, it goes up higher to 67 percent. If mother does not worship, but father does, it is even slightly higher (69 percent). The father has a slightly greater impact than the mother does. If both of them worship, you can see the even larger impact (76 percent).

Figure 9.19. Worshipping with Parents and Teen Virginity

Source: NLS of Ad Health [15]

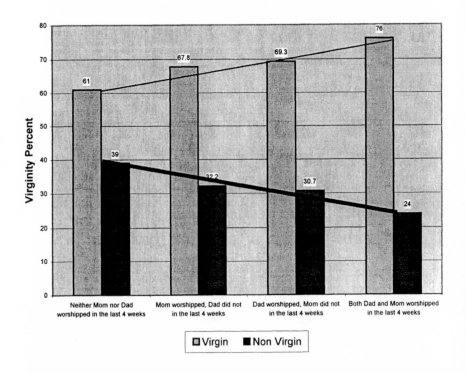

National data for young males in their twenties who did not go to church at all finds very few of them (11.5 percent), who are still virgins (Figure 9.20.). If they go to church infrequently, perhaps once a month, there is a slight rise (16 percent). If they attend two or three times a month, another slight rise (21 percent). If they attended worship once a week or a couple of times a week, it is still higher (38 percent and 54 percent). Clearly, for young men in their twenties, the worship of God has quite an effect on the roving eye and hormones and helps them to be gentlemen, more like sons of God.

Figure 9.20. Young Adult Male Virginity in 1983, Church Attendance in 1982: (NLSY data)

Source: The Heritage Foundation [16]

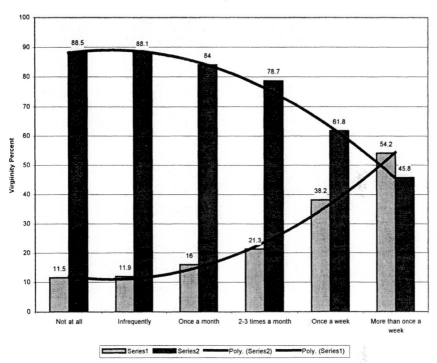

If we consider the peers of sixteen-year-olds and whether or not they are sexually active, we get one of those rare graphs in the social sciences where it is almost a straight line. Consider the data regarding virginity and whether or not they or their friends go to church (Figure 9.21.). If you note those who do not go to church and who have friends who are mostly sexually involved, the chances of such a teenager being a virgin are very slim (4 percent). Or said differently, 96 percent of the time, they would have given up their virginity.

As we move to the middle of the graph, we have some who go to church some of the time and some of their friends are sexually involved. Their chances of being a virgin are about 50 percent. If they go to church regularly each week and their friends are not sexually involved, their chances of being a virgin are 97 percent. So peers have a tremendous impact, which of course, wise parents understand. They cannot control the behavior of the peers, but they try to shepherd their children toward good peers.

Patrick Fagan

Figure 9.21. Loss of Virginity, Peers, and Teenager's Own Worship

Source: E Jeffrey Hill; Brent C. Miller, Maria C Norton, Margaret H. Young [17]

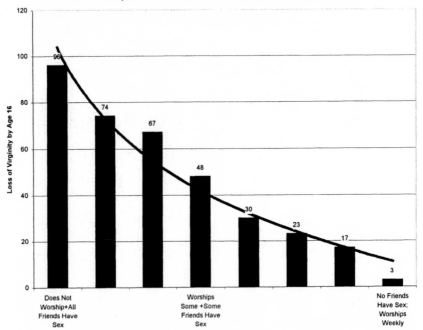

There are two major issues to determine what is happening to children in the United States. One is whether or not the mother and father who brought them into existence are together raising them. Second is whether or not they are worshiping God. The more you combine those two factors, the more you provide for children to grow up well.

In the right-to-life debate, one of the things that has occurred to me that I have never heard discussed is that from the moment of conception, even before the child's existence is threatened or before the mother even knows it is alive, is the right every child has to the love and attention of the man and woman who have just brought him or her into existence. The child has the right to the married love of its parents. That is, a right, and we have seen what happens when it is not there.

Because of the absence of this America is a very dangerous place for children to be conceived. Thirty-three percent are not going to exit their mother's womb. Of those born, 33 percent will be born out of wedlock. Of the rest, about 50 percent will see their mother and father split up before they become adults. I realize that this is a very delicate realm, because every one of us is affected by our faults in this area. So I am not blaming, just describing. But obviously our current culture does not strengthen our children. Rather it is weakening them, the next generation of the United States.

There is no way that we can remain the leading nation of the world and continue on this route. We are collapsing. If you think we are in bad shape, it is instructive to consider Europe. Europe is dying. I don't know if you know it, but Spain and Italy—Catholic Europe—is leading the collapse. Zero population growth is 2.1 children per woman. That average gives you an unchanging population. Spain has 1.1 children per woman. Italy has 1.2. China, properly excoriated for its forced abortion policy, is almost at replacement, at 1.9, a huge and positive difference.

In fifty years' time, the average child in Spain will not have brothers or sisters, aunts or uncles, or cousins. Only the state will be left to hold the nation together. Germany and France, with around 1.4 or 1.5, are also diminishing. To match this major demographic currently unfolding in Europe, we have to go back to the third and fourth centuries when the Vandals, the Huns, and the Visigoth's moved in. Then, they were pushing their way in. Today, in Europe, there is a vacuum pulling them in from North Africa and the Middle East.

On the opposite side is Ireland. I was home in Ireland last November and witnessed one of the leading booming economies of the world. They have enjoyed an average growth rate of 7 to 8 percent per year for the last ten years and have the highest fertility rate in Europe. In fact, Ireland is planning to import labor in the future. But while Ireland has the highest fertility rate, Europe is not replacing itself. We are close to replacement in the U.S., mainly because of our immigrants. Without our immigrants' fertility, America's rate is much the same as France and Germany.

Finally, the reason I switched from clinical psychology with children and families, which I loved doing, was that I saw what was happening in public policy. When I started in clinical work, my patients were mainly children who were referred by pediatricians. In my first year, as I was seeing children, I gradually realized that most of what was happening to the children was in large measure a reaction to what was happening in their families. So I studied and became trained in family therapy. And after about a year-and-a-half of that, I realized that most of what was happening in the family was in large measure a reaction to what was happening between mother and father. So, by my fourth year, when the child was referred to me, I normally set things up so that I got the whole family together, and, as quickly as I could, I peeled off mom and dad. And then we got to work with whatever was going on between them. In about 90 percent of the cases, as they got better, lo and behold, the child spontaneously got better as well.

There is an important insight that has gradually dawned on me over the last year as I put together the data I had collected about the relationship between God, man, marriage, and children. (I am speaking as a Christian here, but those who are not Christian can read between the lines because this actually applies to all faiths.) What has dawned on me is God's purpose. If you consider the profound themes of the scriptures—God creating the world, the creation of Adam and Eve, then the Fall and the Redemption, God the Son becoming man, the Incarnation, Calvary, the resurrection, the founding of the Church and everything since then right through to the end of time, the last days, the last coming, and the final judgment—all of that is in preparation for something. That something is that God has a very clear purpose in mind. He is a father who wants one big family with Him forever in heaven.

How does that big family come into existence? It is through the sexual act. And each one of us comes into existence through the sexual act. So this whole massive design God has is intimately connected to this issue.

The key datum to remember of all that I have covered about American men and women is that most cannot stand each other enough to raise the children they have brought into existence. And government is absolutely incompetent to correct that. But the data are also quite clear. If men and women worship God, God has the power to correct it.

Notes

1. Patrick F. Fagan, "The Breakdown of the Family: The Consequences for Children and American Society," in Heritage Foundation's *Issues 98: Candidate Briefing Book*, ed. Stuart M. Butler and Kim R. Holmes (Washington, D.C.: Heritage Foundation, 1998), 167. Available online at www.heritage.org/issues/98/chap6.html (March 2000).

2. Analysis of National Longitudinal Study of Adolescent Health data performed for the Heritage Foundation by Robert Lerner.

3. Analysis of National Longitudinal Survey of Youth data performed by the Heritage Foundation.

4. Patrick F. Fagan, "How Broken Families Rob Children of Their Choices for Future Prosperity," *Heritage Foundation Backgrounder*, no. 1283 (Washington, D.C.: Heritage Foundation, 11 June 1999), 2.

5. Fagan, "How Broken Families Rob Children of Their Choices for Future Prosperity," 2.

6. Fagan, "How Broken Families Rob Children of Their Choices for Future Prosperity," 2.

7. Heritage Foundation calculations based on Stanley K. Henshaw et al., "Characteristics and Private Contraceptive Use of U.S. Abortion Patients," *Family Planning Perspectives* 20, no. 4 (July/August 1988): 162, and on information provided by the Alan Guttmacher Institute. See also Fagan in *Issues 98: Candidate Briefing Book*, 170.

8. Fagan, "How Broken Families Rob Children of Their Choices for Future Prosperity," 12.

9. Fagan, "How Broken Families Rob Children of Their Choices for Future Prosperity," 6.

10. Patrick F. Fagan and Robert Rector, "The Effects of Divorce on America," *Heritage Foundation Backgrounder*, no. 1373 (Washington, D.C.: Heritage Foundation, 5 June 2000), 9.

11. Fagan and Rector, 12.

12. Fagan and Rector, 7.

13. Fagan and Rector, 5.

14. Patrick F. Fagan, "The Breakdown of the Family: The Consequences for Children and American Society," in Heritage Foundation's *Issues 98: Candidate Briefing Book*,

ed. Stuart M. Butler and Kim R. Holmes (Washington D.C.: Heritage Foundation, 1998), 186. Available online at www.heritage.org/issues/98/chap6.html (March 2000).

15. Patrick F. Fagan and Robert Rector, "Religion: Building Strong Families and Communities," in *Issues 2000: The Candidate's Briefing Book*, ed. Stuart M. Butler and Kim R. Holmes (Washington, D.C.: Heritage Foundation, 2000), 373. Available online at www.heritage.org/issues/chap10.html (March 2000).

16. Analysis of National Longitudinal Survey of Youth data performed by the Heritage Foundation.

17. E. Jeffrey Hill, Thom Curtis, Brent C. Miller, Maria C. Norton, Paul Schvaneveldt, and Margaret H. Young, "The Timing of Sexual Intercourse among Adolescents," *Youth and Society* 29, no. 1 (September 1997): 54-83.

Chapter 10

Status Report on School Vouchers

Douglas W. Kmiec

Every child is unique. Every family is too. Families have distinct histories, occupations, and religious commitments. Yet, from the standpoint of cultural harmony, there must be respect for those things which bind us together. There must be a desire to advance the common welfare, the common good. In a recent book, *Cease-Fire on the Family*,[1] I discuss what I call the culturally determinative mega-virtues of belief in God and a knowable truth. When the public school system took hold in the nineteenth century, it was evident that many fine teachers thought the system would nourish exactly these mega-virtues and instill in children what is today called civic virtue. Unfortunately, there is some evidence in the late nineteenth century that this noble pursuit became partially distorted by bias and fears generated by the large influx of Catholic and Jewish immigrants. These "foreign" people had to be "Americanized," sometimes in ways that were quite unmindful and disrespectful of ethnic and religious cultures. While this is not the place to trace the history of the public schools, it is clear that part of the public school philosophy, at least with respect to these newly arrived Americans, was to separate family and education. It was not a complete separation, however, because the early public school philosophy still adhered to the mega-virtues, and those virtues were largely compatible, or at least not inconsistent, at a more general (if Protestantly flavored) level with the particular ethnic and religious ancestries of the families themselves. As one big city mayor reflects, all worked rather well so long as the mega-virtues supplied a type of "'civil religion' [which] provided the structure for a sound educational system, built on principles the vast majority of Americans would accept."[2] But then came the 1960s, and with it a Supreme Court jurisprudence that raised the wall of separation between church and state to exclusionary proportions. Nowhere was this felt more strongly than in the public school system. As understood by the Court, a nation founded on belief in God suddenly could not draw any distinction based on God. As one constitutional law professor observed: "It [did] not seem to bother the Court that this suspension of judgement on the existence of God results in a governmental preference of agnosticism, which is now recognized by the Court as a non-theistic religion."[3]

Today, we are still a nation of believers, though of many religions. In light of this pluralism of belief, there *is* merit in the Court's decisions insofar as they prevent the coercion of religious belief or practice under penalty of law. But, that said, whatever is the justifiable extent of church-state separation, that separation must not be allowed by families to create greater distance between their particular religious faith and the education of their children. This is especially true now in the midst of cultural hostility because for a family of believers, a genuine religious commitment can mean the difference between educational success and failure.

Enrolling children in a religiously affiliated school helps in two ways: first, the very fact of the affiliation makes the school an extension of the family. They fly under the same flag as it were. Within this shared religious community of family and school, student educational achievement tends to surpass that obtainable in a public or nonreligious private school.[4] Second, the substance of religious instruction itself is frequently of considerable assistance to the development of personal virtue and social responsibility. Both points are discussed more fully below.

Educational Competency

The educational success story of religious schools has been documented most prominently with respect to Catholic parochial (or parish) schools, but the results are not faith-specific. A good summary of this research can be found in a recent book published by Harvard University Press.[5] As summarized there with abundant empirical data, students in religious schools have significantly lower dropout rates and higher verbal and mathematical achievement scores.

While the empirical research of school choice pilot programs is still limited, the prevailing view documented in the Harvard Program on Educational Policy and Governance suggests that they coincide with the more general positive results in private religious schools.[6] For example, in the Milwaukee voucher experiment, the Harvard researchers found that math scores of choice students were 5 to 12 percent higher for third- and fourth-year school choice participants and reading scores were, on average, 3 to 5 percent higher after a similar duration. Under the Ohio pilot scholarship (or choice) program, there was a noticeably high retention rate for inner-city disadvantaged minority children and substantial gains in the early primary grades in reading (5.5 percent higher) and mathematics (15 percent higher).

It appears that the secret of this success is not better facilities, resources, or the self-selection of better students. Almost uniformly, religious schools and those chosen within pilot scholarship programs operate on a fraction of the money available in public schools. For example, in one state it was recently reported that Catholic schools spend thirty-five hundred dollars or less per student compared with a state average of ten-thousand dollars per student in the public school system. As for the argument that religious schools "skim" the best and the brightest, the claim, according to researchers, "cannot withstand examination." For example, one Michigan study found that "students who attend Detroit area private schools reflect the surrounding geographical areas which by and large were relatively poor, low-income and in some cases middle-income areas."[7]

By now, it is well known that national study commissions have singled out public education as "eroded by a rising tide of mediocrity that threatens our very future as a Nation and a people."[8] Our own national self-assessment now appears validated by international comparison. In recent international competitions announced in late February 1998, American twelfth-graders scored well below the world average in the Third International Mathematics and Science Study (TIMSS).[9] No country ranked lower than the United States in student performance in advanced mathematics and physics. On the assessment of math general knowledge, the U.S. score was 461. Hungary, Germany, Slovenia, Austria, Canada, Australia, New Zealand, France, Norway, Iceland, Switzerland, Denmark, Sweden, and the Netherlands had significantly higher average scores than the United States. The highest score was 560 in the Netherlands. Similarly, on the assessment of science general knowledge, the U.S. average score was 480. Denmark, Slovenia, Austria, Switzerland, Australia, New Zealand, Canada, Norway, Iceland, the Netherlands, and Sweden had significantly higher average scores than the United States. The highest score was 559 in Sweden. The latest tests showed American high school seniors to finish nineteenth out of the twenty-one nations participating, and the testing regimen did not include traditionally high-performing Asian nations.

Earlier international comparisons in the late 1980s were much the same. American students on nineteen academic tests never finished first or second and, "when compared with other industrialized nations, were last seven times."[10] On most standardized tests, the average achievement of high school students is less than the comparable student thirty years ago. When the National Geographic Society tested eighteen to twenty-four-year-olds, the *New York Times* reported that America finished dead last among the ten nations tested, with even 14 percent of the Americans unable to find the United States on a world map.[11]

Moral Formation

A complete education must involve more than basic competencies or the acquisition of skills; it must also aid in the formation of moral character. The success or failure of America as a government, and as a democratically organized culture, depends upon the moral development of its people, and especially its school children. That is why the Northwest Ordinance of 1787, the governing document shaping the early territorial expansion of the United States, deliberately linked "religion, morality, and knowledge [as] being necessary to good government and the happiness of mankind." From the view of America's founding generation, religion and education were inseparable. Is there reason to conclude that this is no longer true today?

The moral formation side of the education equation in many public schools is little better. A few years ago, government statistics revealed that *each* month close to three-hundred thousand students and more than five-thousand teachers were attacked in public schools.[12] It is frightfully commonplace for school administrators to discover students carrying weapons. As the late Chief Justice Warren Burger lamented, "Days in school with dedicated teachers and eager students struggling to master their lessons have given way, all too often, to disorder and a gripping fear by teachers and students."[13] Obviously, this increased level of violence and disruption in public schools only aggravates the decline in academic achievement and makes more remote any chance for its reversal.[14] Among other things, school violence rationally convinces some to avoid coming to school entirely, an invitation all too willingly accepted by marginal students.[15]

Religiously affiliated schools accept far less bad behavior before bringing in parents or exacting academic penalties. Because these schools are not arms of the government, it is still possible for discipline to be imposed without triggering claims that some constitutional right has been violated, such as legal rights to formal notice and hearing, counsel, or a dispassionate, disinterested decision-maker. Yet, the superior achievement and moral advantage of religious schools is attributable to more than procedural flexibility. In particular, it is most traceable to the fact that "the religious affiliation is *shared* by parent, child and school."[16]

Educational Achievement and Moral Formation— The Outgrowth of Uniting Family and School

Research comparing public and religious schools reveals that the best outputs in terms of student achievement are far less related to what is spent on education than the existence of a religious community tying family and school together. This shared religious affiliation results in the close and continuing involvement of parents, and this "social capital" means far more to academic success than the financial capital of either the family (whether they are rich or poor) or the school institution (including teacher salaries or the school's library and facilities). Surprisingly, the "social capital" of the shared religious affiliation even appears to overcome "input" weaknesses in the family structure itself. In this respect, University of Chicago sociologist Dr. James Coleman found that children in religiously affiliated schools from single-parent households or where both parents work were also less likely than their public school counterparts to drop out of school. In Dr. Coleman's sociologist words, "The social capital in the religious community surrounding the school appears especially effective for those children lacking strong social capital within the family."[17]

The continued involvement of parents in the religious community that surrounds a religious school encourages the child's unique potential in ways that cannot be duplicated in most public school classrooms. It also ensures greater supervision of the child's individual effort and the accountability of his or her instructors. In essence, the religious affiliation invites the extension of the family into the school. In this way, parents remain the ultimate guarantors against their children becoming lost in the crowd or, if you will, standardized. Despite the confusions of its church-state cases, the Supreme Court long ago formally recognized the preeminent parental role in education. The Court wrote: "The child is not the mere creature of the State; those [parents] who nurture him and direct his destiny have the right, coupled with the high duty, to recognize and prepare him for additional obligations."[18]

The preeminence of the parental role, of course, must not be abused. When we speak of maintaining a strong connection between family and school, and especially a family's religious tradition and school, it is not a license to instill antisocial beliefs. But by the same token, it is an overstatement to insist that separate Hebrew and Catholic and Lutheran and Evangelical and Pentecostal and Baptist schools tear at the American fabric. Indeed, quite the opposite is true. Allowing the freedom for these religious groupings to flourish is the very pattern of the American fabric. Attempts to submerge the separate manner in which Americans freely choose to worship God, and to educate themselves and their families in conformity with religious belief, will only leave the national fabric bleached and ill-fitting.

For parents choosing a religious school, instruction in matters of basic knowledge is not artificially divided from specific guidance toward personal responsibility. The child is not uncomfortably forced to live two lives—one at home and the other at school. Most importantly, the child is not pressured into abandoning one or the other source of teaching. Parental instruction is reaffirmed and elaborated by the religious school. The health of our culture depends on far more than the minimalist objective of keeping guns out of the classroom or the certification of vague "opportunity to learn standards" by the U.S. Department of Education under the so-called Goals 2000 Educate America Act.[19]

The famed educator, Rudolf Steiner, credited with identifying the importance of early childhood education, stated it in these eloquent terms:

If one observes children who, by right upbringing, have developed a natural reverence for the grownups in their surroundings, and if one follows them through their various stages of life, one can discover that their feelings of reverence and devotion in childhood are gradually being transformed during the years leading to old age. As adults such persons may have a healing effect upon their fellow-men so that by a single glance they can spread inner peace to others. Their presence can be a blessing because as children they have learned to venerate and to pray in the right way. No hands can bless in old age, unless in childhood they have been folded in prayer.[20]

Douglas W. Kmiec

The Unnecessary Separation of
Family Religion from Education

So why, then, is the family's religion separated from education? The simple answer, suggested earlier, is the difficulty the Supreme Court has had reconciling the constitutional provision barring the establishment of religion with religion's obvious connection to the type of moral instruction that must occur in school if the school is faithfully to be the extension or teaching agent of parents. The Constitution has been construed to require freedom from, not freedom of, religion. A proper wall of separation between church and state is improperly employed to drive an unnecessary and unwise wedge between parent and child in terms of education. That has been done elsewhere.[21] Here, I merely wish to address how the damage done by this wedge is aggravated when public resources for education are taxed away from the family and directed to only one educational provider.

There is no good amelioration for this damage short of allowing parents to choose, freely, the school that their children will attend. It is too late in the day to pretend that the public schools can return to some pre-1960s form of homogenized, Protestant moral instruction that may have then infused the school system. Nor would such a return be desirable, as multi-denominational religious instruction is incoherent or shallow. A few members of Congress have vainly sought to return down this path by suggesting laws that would mandate the teaching of generic values without religion. Besides being the equivalent of teaching flying without a plane, these proposals hit a snag the moment someone asks what values are to be taught or how they are to be defined and why. Because of this, seven times during recent years, Congress has been unable to agree on offering meager demonstration grants to promote honesty, responsibility, and even something insipidly labeled "caring." A few local communities have had better luck in getting past the definitional stage because the values of their local community were still sufficiently tangible and shared within these smaller geographical settings to be identified. However, for Congress to attempt this nationally raises all of the problems associated with using law as a substitute for morality, including exacerbated cultural tension and ultimately vapid standards. As Congressman Richard Armey said in opposing one such national effort:

> I for one, would not tolerate anybody having the presumption to dare to think they should define who my children are, what their values are, what their ethics are and who in the hell they will be in this world. The fact is these people don't know my children and the fact is they don't love my children. And the fact is they don't care about my children and the further fact is they accept no responsibility for the outcome . . . and they ought, by God, leave my kids alone.[22]

Congressman Armey's words have great intensity and, in my judgment, underscore the reasons why parents must directly and freely choose their children's schools: Teachers come and go while parents love children always; parents must be free to manifest that love through one of the most important gifts they can supply—namely, their specific religious tradition.

The One-Sided Funding of Public Schools

It may be argued in response that all parents are presently free to send their children to a religious school; they merely must pay for it. The facetious nature of this asserted "freedom" was aptly rebutted by John Lyon in *The Family in America*, one of the Rockford Institute's excellent publications of assistance to families. Lyon writes:

> Just how "free" would we be to exercise our right to provide nourishing food for our children if the government taxed us to support a state chain of comprehensive supermarkets and required that there be one in every "food district" of the state? We might set up peoples' food co-ops until we were blue, but we could not really compete with the government's subsidized chain. The situation might be minimally tolerable if state stores offered quality goods. But if, in our suppositious case, the government decided to purvey largely junk food in its subsidized supermarkets, the situation would be intolerable.[23]

And while we are on the subject of who is free to do what, let me suggest that the notion that has taken hold that it is constitutionally permissible to tax all citizens to create a common fund for education, but to then exclude some citizens on the basis of religious belief is a gross disregard for the principles of free exercise of religion embodied by the First Amendment (even if this principle is presently slighted in case law). This unjust and unequal treatment is no more sustainable than if the government set aside tax monies for cancer research and then pronounced that Lutheran or Baptist physicians, or more broadly any person of faith, need not apply.

Again, it may be claimed that religionists are not excluded from public funds; the government is merely declining to subsidize the constitutional freedom to go to a religious school. There is some facial plausibility to this argument. It falls away, however, as Lyon points out above, when it is recognized that there are different ways to deny freedom, including the very practical one of making families pay twice (especially those with limited resources) to act on their religious convictions (once to the government in taxes and once to the private school).

Others may try to finesse the troublesome exclusion of believers from their own money in the public education fund by denying the premise—that is, that attendance at a public school burdens religious belief or practice. This may be true for some families; they could have their children attend the public school without formally transgressing church instruction. For others, however, this is not the case, as readings or other class exercises directly contravene church teaching.[24] As one Christian medical doctor explained "a child left to himself [in a public school] will not choose the path to Christ without some direction from persons of significance around him."[25] In any event, Supreme Court justices ought not sit in judgment of what any person's religious belief requires, unless public order is directly threatened. The justices have said as much themselves.[26] For example, the Supreme Court has held that a person cannot be forced to choose between following the dictates of her religion and a government benefit, such as unemployment compensation.[27] Remembering, too, that the Court has confirmed the right of parents, not the state, to direct their children's education, it is insupportable to make parents choose between their religion and the only available public support for education in the form of the public school.

In Funding Education, Let Parents be Parents

The solution for reuniting education and family in the pursuit of virtue is obvious: Tax monies for education must once again be brought under direct family control. The proposition that public resources ought to be distributed evenhandedly without discrimination is well established in law—except, that is, in the area of education. Educational dollars contributed *by all* taxpayers remain, at present, available only to *some*. Why is that?

The issue of school choice has been around so long, one wonders why we have not sent those opposing it home for remedial instruction. The reasons for perpetuating discrimination against taxpaying parents with children in private and religious schools are fast disappearing. On the legal front, the government has no business coercing religious belief or practice, but teaching long division or phonics in a religious school classroom is hardly that. In *Agostini v. Felton*,[28] decided in 1997, the Supreme Court "repudiated" earlier views to the contrary.

But more importantly, the Court also distanced itself from the longtime bugaboo that any and all public aid that directly assists the general educational function of religious schools impermissibly finances religious instruction. This is silly, said the Court, since disbursing public grant money to parents for use at the school of their choice is no different than a state employee freely donating part of her state salary to her local church. "In both situations, any money that ultimately [goes] to religious institutions [does] so only as a result of the genuinely independent and private choices of individuals."

Justice Souter in dissent floated a newly invented distinction between a small amount of public money to children attending religious schools and greater sums like those that would likely be entailed by a voucher or scholarship program. Not a wall of separation, one might say, but a picket fence. The Court properly saw such microeconomic line-drawing to be wholly artificial. The constitutionality of an educational program, it concluded, should not depend on the number of religious school students who happen to receive neutrally available assistance.

While *Agostini*, itself, did not involve a voucher program, its reasoning strongly suggests that a carefully drafted one allowing parents to allocate their own tax money to the school of their choice would survive federal constitutional scrutiny. The Court has acknowledged that generally available public funding may reach religious schools if it is directed there by the choices of individual parents.[29] When individual parents are making the decisions about how to spend their own funds, it cannot be seriously argued that it is the state that is endorsing or establishing religion.

But now state laws are being used to obstruct the way. Recognizing this, the Washington-based Institute for Justice has made school choice the civil rights issue of the 1990s, leading the litigation effort in Wisconsin, Ohio, Vermont, Maine, and elsewhere.

And parents are taking notice. A 1997 study for the Joint Center for Political and Economic Studies, for example, found high interest across parent populations but particularly intense attraction from the urban poor. In a similar nationwide survey conducted by Stanford, 79 percent of inner-city residents favored a school voucher plan.

The very positive response from the most disadvantaged should scarcely be surprising. Unlike President Clinton and more affluent families who can afford the double tuition bill to send their children to private schools, low income and, often, minority families have no escape. Nevertheless, voucher opponents misleadingly insist that giving private school parents their fair share of the public education fund will either result in racial stratification or leave private schools beyond the economic reach of most.

Published data, some from the government itself, belie these canards. Department of Education reports, for instance, indicate that private schools are less racially exclusive than the public schools in the communities in which they are located. Nor is there any truth to the tired argument about the supposed inadequacy of voucher levels to pay private school tuition. Washington's Cato Institute pegs the average private school tuition at $3,116, less than half the national average cost to educate a student in public school ($6,857).

Choice is not a cure-all, but the performance results from the Milwaukee and Ohio programs are encouraging. In particular, students from the most economically disadvantaged homes given a choice of schools are scoring higher on mathematics and reading tests than their public school counterparts. While education researchers rightly caution that the favorable effects of school choice occur gradually over time, often after three to four years, the percentile jumps in math and reading performance are hard to dismiss.

Conclusion

School choice is not antipublic school. As the father of five children, some of whom attend public school, I know of many truly excellent public school classrooms and teachers. Choice advocates, by definition, want what the word describes—additional options. It is not who owns the school that matters necessarily, but whether the school provides a well-thought-out program of instruction,

② reasonable discipline, and a hard-working staff not encumbered by an educational bureaucracy. As discussed herein, of vital importance is whether there are ample opportunities for parental involvement—something which a shared religious base facilitates.

For every child, a family remains the best teacher. When families find meaning in religious faith, it is highly preferable and advantageous if educational agents outside the home can draw upon that faith too. Separation of church and state properly does keep government out of the tenets of faith and, by the same token, particular religious dogma out of government policy. Today, however, separation of church and state is being improperly used to separate family from education. America's religious freedom does not depend upon either diminishing the primary role of parents as the moral educators of their children or inhibiting family religious commitment. In truth, the restoration of America's cultural virtue depends on just the opposite.

So who exactly is blocking the school house door? Whomever, it is long past time to step aside and let all parents direct the upbringing of their children by allocating their share of the general public education fund to the school of their choice.

Notes

1. Portions of this discussion are derived from this volume. Douglas W. Kmiec, *Cease-Fire on the Family and the End of the Culture War* (Notre Dame, Ind.: Crisis Books, 1995).

2. Philip F. Lawler, "Breaking the Logjam?" *The Catholic World Report* (July 1994): 44.

3. Charles E. Rice, "We Hold No Truths?" *Triumph* (September 1968): 11, 13.

4. James S. Coleman, "The Creation and Destruction of Social Capital: Implications for the Law," 3 *Notre Dame J. of L. and Pub. Pol.* 375 (1988) [hereinafter "Coleman"]. Cf., Coleman and colleagues concluded that family and peers were generally more influential on student performance than schools. See generally, J. Coleman, E. Campbell, C. Hobson, J. Mcpartland, A. Mood, F. Weinfield, & R. York, *Equality of Educational Opportunity* (1966) and later related work, James S. Coleman, Thomas Hoffer, and Sally Kilgore, *High School Achievement: Public, Catholic, and Private Schools Compared* (New York: Basic Books, 1982), 193.

5. Anthony S. Byrk, Valerie E. Lee, and Peter B. Holland, *Catholic Schools and the Common Good* (Cambridge, Mass.: Harvard, 1993).

6. The papers from the Harvard project are collected online at data.fas.harvard.edu/pepg/ (April 1998).

7. Harry Hutchinson, "Private Schools: Let Competition Heat Up," in *Educational Choice for Michigan*, Mackinac Center Report (September 1991), 57.

8. *A Nation at Risk*, The National Commission on Excellence in Education (Washington, D.C.: Government Printing Office, 1983), 5.

9. Carrol Innerst, "High School Seniors Land in Math, Science Cellar; U.S. Ranks 19th in 21-Nation Survey," *Washington Times*, 25 February 1998, A1.

10. The Mackinac Center Report, citing the National Commission on Excellence in Education.

11. The Mackinac Center Report, citing the *New York Times* of November 9, 1989.

12. *National School Safety Center News Journal* (winter 1987).

13. Warren Burger, "School Safety Goes to Court," *School Safety* (winter 1986): 4-5.

14. National Institute of Justice, *Violence in Schools* (December 1986), 2.

15. See Gregory L. Evans, "School Crime and Violence: Achieving Deterrence through Tort Law," 3 *Notre Dame J. of Law and Pub. Pol.* 375 (1988).

16. James S. Coleman, "The Creation and Destruction of Social Capital: Implications for the Law," 3 *Notre Dame J. of L. and Pub. Pol.* (1988): 375.

17. Coleman, supra at 382.

18. *Pirece v. Society of Sisters*, 268 U.S. 510 (1925).

19. *Bruno v. Manno*, "Outcome-Based Education–Miracle Cure or Plague?" *Hudson Briefing Paper* (No. 165, June 1994), 10.

20. Rudolf Steiner, *The Renewal of Education* (Herndon, Virg.: Anthroposophic Press, 1981), 65.

21. See Douglas W. Kmiec, *The Attorney General's Lawyer* (1992); see also, Douglas W. Kmiec and Stephen B. Presser, *The American Constitutional Order* (Cincinnati, Ohio: Anderson Publishing, 1999), Ch. 2.

22. Rochelle Sharpe, "Efforts to Promote Teaching of Values in Schools Are Sparking Heated Debate Among Lawmakers," *Wall Street Journal* (10 May 1994), A20.

23. John Lyon, "Reclaiming the Schools: Reconciling Home and Education," 8 *The Family in America*, (No. 6, June 1994), 6.

24. *Mozert v. Hawkins*, 827 F. 2d 1058 (sixth Cir. 1987), cert. Den., *Mozert v. Hawkins County Public Schools*, 484 U.S. 1066, 108 S.Ct. 1029, 98 L.Ed.2d 993, 44 Ed. Law Rep. 1000 (U.S. Tenn., Feb 22, 1988) (No. 87-1100).

25. William Sears, *Christian Parenting and Child Care* (Nashville: Thos. Nelson, 1991): 410.

26. *Employment Division v. Smith*, 494 U.S. 872 (1990).

27. *Shubert v. Verner*, 374 U.S. 398 (1963).

28. 117 S.Ct. 1997 (1997).

29. *Mueller v. Allen*, 463 U.S. 388 (1983); *Witters v. Washington State Department of Services for the Blind*, 474 U.S. 481 (1986); *Zobrest v. Catalina Foothills School District*, 509 U.S. 1 (1993).

Chapter 11

A Family-Friendly Tax System

Charles Van Eaton

There are two dimensions where our nation's policies affecting American families have worked not for the better, but for the worse. The first has to do with how the growth of the welfare state has changed our culture's view of what the family is and what responsibilities attach to it. The second is a product of the failure to address the way in which the federal income tax system has forced many families with children, particularly small children, to reduce the time available for the daily care and nurturing of children because of the need for both parents to work outside the home.

First, the moral dimension: In a letter to Ann Landers, a daughter-in-law had a message for all mothers-in-law: "Just because you took care of your old senile mother doesn't mean you have the right to expect us to take care of you. It's time you learned that this is a new age and things are different."

Indeed, it is a new age and things are different. But are they better? This woman seems to think that if Social Security checks are coming to her mother-in-law, she is automatically relieved of any moral responsibility. Her willingness to let the state substitute for family has made her morally numb.

The Social Security Act of 1935 was not intended to be an aggressive government seizure of fundamental family functions. While it took several decades for this system to drive a wedge through the cross-generational obligations (i.e., parents caring for children and, later, children caring for elderly parents) which once characterized American families and which did much to educate children within the family setting, by 1980 the Social Security-driven separation of one generation from another was virtually complete. Whereas in 1957, some twenty-one years after passage of the Social Security Act, 52.5 percent of persons over age sixty-five received some financial support from their children and/or lived with their children and grandchildren, by 1980 only 4 percent received some aid from their children or lived with their children (in fact, twice as many of the elderly routinely provided financial aid to their adult children).[1]

The woman who wrote to Ann Landers is a product of that system.

For several decades evidence has grown to suggest that we have become a nation in which the family, the single most civilizing force known to human-kind, has become harder to establish and maintain. "Changing family structure is the greatest long-term threat to U.S. children," concludes a team of researchers from [Pennsylvania State University in 1989. They reported] that while nine out of ten children living above the poverty line lived in a two-parent family, most of the nation's poor children lived in a single-parent, female-headed household.[2]

John DiIulio has further confirmed that these trends lead to increased crime committed by children. The National Institute of Justice reports that the number of violent crimes committed by persons under the age of eighteen has more than doubled in the past twenty years. Teenagers commit more than half of all mur-ders. Social scientist Wade Mackey's ongoing research on the root causes of violent crime concludes, "There is no statistical relationship between violent crime and joblessness, but there is a robust statistical relationship between vio-lent crime rates and the percentage of all children born to single mothers: more illegitimacy translates into more violent crime."[3] Author and social critic Charles Murray further notes that the best single predictor of future poverty, crime, ignorance, educational dysfunction, homelessness, drug addiction, and every other social pathology is the growth in the number of female-headed, sin-gle-parent households.[4]

Some suggest that government programs should be enacted to correct all this. Surely, they reason, activist policies could provide childcare for working parents, tax subsidies for families caring for elderly parents, and financial aid for single mothers so they can stay at home with their children. After all, we are a rich nation and we can do anything.

Charles Murray has long argued that government assistance makes matters absolutely worse. He poses two questions:

> Suppose we fight poverty and poverty rates go down, as such rates are offi-cially measured. If this is accompanied by an increase in the number of children born to single women, is our nation actually doing better or worse? Suppose food stamps were so readily available that no young man who contributed to the conception of a child ever had to worry about that child having enough to eat. Would that be the best of all possible worlds for that child?[5]

Over the past fifty years we have seen a continual expansion in government programs which have effectively absorbed functions traditionally the responsi-bility of families and churches. Along with this growth in government programs has come a steady growth in crime, seemingly intractable poverty across genera-tions, and the loss of any sense of moral obligation of children for older parents and parents for children.

One would do well to ask if government could actually solve family prob-lems at any level. The answer hinges on what one means by the word "family." If the family is whatever current social and moral norms dictate, and if this in-cludes a wide variety of arrangements among consenting adults, then the phrase "family problems" ceases to have any real meaning separate and apart from human problems in general. Therefore, if the political sector can generate programs which "solve" human problems, it can "solve" family problems. But if the term "family" defines something unique, something distinct from autonomous individuals on the one hand and society on the other hand, family problems become important. Indeed, they become so important that, if left unsolved, society itself could be threatened.

Some have argued that the so-called traditional nuclear family is nothing more than a spontaneous and evolutionary social arrangement which came into being only because it did a better job of helping individuals survive than did some alternative system. If social and economic conditions change enough to allow the "unconnected" individual to survive, if not prosper, the "traditional" family has no moral claim on society in general or any one person in particular.

This latter view of the family is one supported by Professor Marvin Sussman of the University of Delaware and historian Stephanie Coontz, author of *The Way We Never Were: American Families and the Nostalgia Trap.*[6] The family, they argue, is whatever individuals choose it to be and nothing more.

But this view of the family is not only at variance with the Judeo-Christian tradition (the "Western" tradition), it is at variance with history as well. As Professors Brigitte and Peter Berger of Boston University have forcefully argued, the traditional and autonomous nuclear family is as old as human history and records of its existence have been found across every culture and every form of economic organization. Indeed, they argue, its moral and economic health predicts the economic, social, and moral health of society in general.

Early in the history of the Hebrew nation, there was a rebellion against the single rule of God and the prominence of the nuclear family with all its attendant responsibilities. This rebellion took the form of a call for establishing a civil government with a king who would exercise sovereignty even over families. In response to this plea, the prophet told the people they could have their king, but (and this was a clear economic argument) with it they would have to be prepared not only to give up their material resources, but their sons and daughters as well. As the influence of the civil authority grew and became a center of power in competition with the family, the influence and claims of the family would be gradually weakened.

Some seven-hundred years after this event, the Greek philosopher Plato wrote that the state was due more honor than the family. This assertion was essential to his theory of the Republic because he knew that the state could expand only to the extent that the family could be made irrelevant to future generations. Clearly this view, in one form or another, still exists. But, just as clearly, it is at odds with an alternative view of the family and, for that matter, the world as well.

In the Judeo-Christian tradition, the family is first—prior to both society in general and the state in particular. Indeed, in the Judeo-Christian tradition, there has always been tension between the state and the family. While the New Testament taught Christians that they were to pay their taxes, obey the laws, and give honor to those who exercised civil authority over them, they were also taught, as were their predecessors in Old Testament times, that government was not something which could or should be used to relieve individuals of the responsibility of caring for their own families.

In the Hebrew Bible, men who married were told to leave their father and mother and be bound, as if "one flesh," to their wives. Fathers and mothers were taught to raise their children in the "nurture and admonition" of the Lord. Parents were to be honored, including, as every Bible scholar agrees, caring for them in their old age.

The same moral principles are taught in the Christian Scriptures. Wives were taught to be subject to their husbands, husbands were taught to love and support their wives, and children were to be raised in love and moral discipline. Parents were to be honored for the moral health and economic security of the family and, by implication, the extended community. Fathers were to provide for their own families or face expulsion from the Christian community.

If this view of family is valid, any government program which displaces the family and the internal moral and financial responsibilities which reside in families is wrong—indeed, profoundly immoral.

Second, there is an economic role of policies affecting families which also has moral implications. How, for instance, do current federal tax and income redistribution policies affect families in ways which give rise to the moral problems which lie at the base of family pathology? How has the modern welfare system, recently modified but still omnipresent, impacted both moral and economic issues within the family?

The financial distress which accompanies the moral component of family life relates less to the absence of government programs than to a federal tax system's bias against families with children. This bias was never intentional. Nevertheless, it is real and has been allowed to grow. Consequently, many families which would prefer to have one parent at home to care for and morally nurture their children have been compelled to have both parents employed outside the home. (Those who quickly rush to the argument that educational opportunities have been the major force leading married women with children to work full time are missing a critical fact: The typical working mother is not a lawyer or doctor. She is a clerk, a waitress, or a secretary. She works very hard and, after taxes, takes not a great deal of money home.)

There is a serious problem which can follow the need for mothers to work outside the home. University of Toronto sociologists have found higher rates of delinquency among female teens in single-parent households than in traditional two-parent households. But they have found higher rates of delinquency among female teens in two-parent households where mothers pursued careers which took them away from direct, day-to-day management of the family, regardless of family income.[7]

What change in tax policy can best help the American family? First, we should eliminate the bias which our federal income tax system now has against those who marry and have children. Second, our political leaders must continue the changes to a welfare system which, as Charles Murray and others have argued, essentially subsidizes behavior which produces dysfunctional families.

Despite the 1981 and 1986 federal tax rate reductions, failure to fully adjust the value of the personal exemption in line with inflation and the growth in income since 1948, has resulted in the share of family income paid for income taxes increased to twenty-six times more than was paid in 1948. To shield the same proportion of median family income today as was shielded by the six hundred dollar personal exemption in 1948, the personal exemption would have to be raised to $6,708, thus removing a four-person family earning thirty-two thousand dollars from the federal tax roles. This would grant them the same degree of financial independence a similar median-income family of four enjoyed in 1948. Since the advent of the modern federal income tax system in the 1940s, and despite much tinkering with the tax code, today's families with children are the only segment of society left without any protection from a seemingly insatiable federal government. (Some economists would argue the equivalent exemption should be as high as eight-five hundred dollars.)

Given the rising cost of rearing children and the dramatic real decline in disposable family income which failure to adjust the personal exemption rate has caused, many married women who might have chosen to stay at home, performing the critically essential task of teaching and nurturing their children, have been compelled to enter the job market. Given what is now known about the critical influence of mothers on their children, it surely is better to open this opportunity to those who would choose it rather than to continue a tax system which makes it increasingly difficult.

The second thing government can do to help all American families is to determine that there will be no turning back from the steps taken in the 1996 Welfare Reform Act to stop subsidizing those behaviors which help create dysfunctional families. This means putting an end, as one famous American put it, to "welfare as we know it" and really meaning it.

Eloise Anderson, the product of a black, working-class family in Toledo, Ohio, who served as the head of California's state welfare system, recalls,

> I grew up around people who were poor; I lived next door to and around people on AFDC, so I know the games they play. These people are not inferior, they are not irrational. They know how the system works, what it rewards and what it does not. They know it does not reward people who have husbands and it doesn't reward working. AFDC really changed the conversation between men and women. It deprived poor men of a place in the family. AFDC created itself as the husband, and no poor man could compete with it. It is nothing more than a government-sponsored system of child abuse, and the only way to stop it is to stop pumping in the money.[8]

I can imagine people claiming that children would starve if the welfare door was never opened to newcomers. I would argue that instead there would soon be fewer children born to only one parent and fewer men abandoning their families.

It is no longer possible to dispute the facts: The single best indicator of infant mortality, whether the child will grow up in poverty, how well he will perform in school, and whether he is likely to turn to crime and drugs, is the marital status of his parents. The welfare state has done much to destroy marriage. Indeed, for many women, the welfare state substituted for husband and father. The results are in: The product has been poverty and death.

Hopefully, the welfare reform begun in 1996 will continue. The evidence to this point is that the "culture of poverty" has been broken. Now it has to be acknowledged that the effect of welfare was social pathology. But those who might want to return to the old system should join with all to admit that it was a mistake and must never be repeated.

The family is a sacred institution and men and women who fail to take family obligations seriously are living in opposition to the normative requirements of the Judeo-Christian, Western tradition. America needs a period of confession and repentance if the family is going to be strengthened.

In addition, the federal tax code should be changed to eliminate its current bias against married couples, particularly those who have children. Once we acknowledge that we must eliminate the burden our tax system imposes on families, we should then radically simplify the federal income tax system by eliminating the high progressive rates which now characterize its structure. Finally, government must never again institute the old welfare system—that system which did so much to subsidize those behaviors that weaken family life.

A beginning has been made but the end has not been reached. The task continues.

Notes

1. Calculated from U.S. Census data, various years www.census.gov (March 1998).

2. Patrick Fagan, Heritage Foundation, Washington, D.C. Review of literature cited by Mona Charen, syndicated columnist, 20 March 1995.

3. Charen, citing Fagan.

4. Charles Murray, *Losing Ground: American Social Policy 1950-1980* (Washington, D.C.: Perseus Books, 1995), 119.

5. Charles Murray, interview with Maria Dickenson in "Stopping the Welfare Overflow," *The Detroit News*, 19 January 1993.

6. Stephanie Coontz and Marvin Sussman, *The Way We Never Were: American Families and the Nostalgia Trap* (New York: Basic Books, 1992).

7. Charen, citing Fagan.

8. Carolyn Lochhead. "California's Back to Reality Welfare Reformer," *City Journal* 5, no. 2 (Spring 1995): 56-61. Available online at www.city-journal.org/html/5_2_californias.html (April 1998).

Part V

A Season of Renewal:
Taking It Personally

Chapter 12

Moral Freedom

Alan Wolfe

It is a great pleasure to be here at this wonderfully ecumenical institution called Pepperdine University. Previous speakers have included some of America's most distinguished commentators to speak about the nature of the American condition. I want to begin my remarks by referring to two of them, James Q. Wilson and Michael Novak, both of whom have called our attention to serious problems in the moral character of the United States. They are among a handful of public policy intellectuals who have said that in the United States we are suffering from a kind of serious moral deficit, that the moral character of our country is not what it formerly was. Consequently, the very future of our republic is in serious danger unless we pay close attention to questions of morality and character.

The idea that something is going wrong in the nature of American virtue is of course not an idea we associate only with James Q. Wilson and Michael Novak. William Bennett has contributed much to this idea through his books, especially *The Book of Virtues*. Robert Bork in his book, *Slouching Toward Gomorrah,* has probably made one of the strongest statements of this position. Gertrude Himmelfarb and her husband, Irving Kristol, have both added their voices. This is a very ecumenical statement about the nature of the American soul at this particular moment. It is not confined to people of any particular religious belief. Among the people I have just mentioned, including Protestants, Catholics, and Jews, there are those who are deeply concerned about what we have become.

It is one of the most important questions raised by people who think about what is happening in the United States. But it is also a very troubling question because the United States is a democracy. And because of that, it seems to me, if we say there is something wrong with America, we are saying that there is something fundamentally wrong with Americans, because Americans are America. That is what it means to be a democracy. If the moral character of the country is crumbling or is in serious danger, then something is going on in the inner

125

most hearts of most of the American people. That's troubling. I also find it a difficult question because it does not correspond with the America I know.

Most of the people I know in the United States are good people. They are people who love their country, they are people who love their God, and they are people who are trying their hardest to live as best they can.

How do we square the circle here? How do we point to the kind of evidence that Patrick Fagan brings to our attention—evidence about people? Every statistic and every diagram he presents is about real individuals.

When we talk about marriage, when we talk about divorce, when we talk about childbirth, we are talking about real people. Are we saying that because of the kind of empirical data that we have, these real individuals themselves in some way have gone wrong? It may very well be. But then that is indeed what we must say clearly.

But before we reach that conclusion, I would at least like to add to the conversation one additional voice. That voice is the voice of the American people themselves. I would like to know what they think about their condition. How do they understand morality when they think about the classic questions of virtue and vice? How do they explain themselves? Do they have a moral philosophy about why we human beings are here on the earth? What is our purpose here? What are we living for? And if they do, how would they describe it? What is it? What relationship does that understanding have with some of the great moral and theological traditions which shaped American society?

This is essentially what I do. I spend my time developing research projects that identify people throughout the United States. I write them letters, follow up with phone calls and say, "Hey, I'd like to talk to you. These are the kinds of things that I'm interested in. I'd like to know what you think about morality. I'd like to know what you think about virtue," and "Could we have some of your time? We'll do it any way you want—your house or your workplace—and it will take about an hour and a half. May we come and talk to you?"

The first thing I can tell you is that for all of the talk about how we are now no longer social people, that we "bowl alone," or that we have become excessively narcissistic and individualistic, most people, when approached this way, are absolutely delighted to talk. They want to talk because they are so fed up with being called by telemarketers that they can't quite believe us at first. That is why we send them a letter.

I have shared much of what I have discovered in the book, *One Nation, After All*. Now I am doing it in a new research project in which I'm trying to explore with people what the notion of virtue means. Virtue and vice—what are these terms? Are they in your vocabulary? Are these things that you think about? If you think about them, what do they mean to you? How do you try to live by these principles?

I'd like to give you an initial overview of some of the things that I've been discovering and then see whether or not they have anything to say about the questions about our moral character raised by James Q. Wilson, Michael Novak, Bill Bennett, and others.

One way to fashion the question is to refer to one of the truly great moral contemporary philosophers in America, Alasdair MacIntyre. His book, *After Virtue,* is, I think, the single best statement of the idea that something is going wrong with our character. One of the main things he says in his book is that Americans, and by Americans he means modern western people living in societies like the United States, essentially no longer even have conceptions like virtue in their vocabulary. In a sense they don't even know what the words mean. That should be easily tested. You just ask people, "What does virtue mean?" You find out whether it's in their vocabulary or not. Then I can immediately tell you whether Alasdair MacIntyre is right or wrong. And the answer is, he's right.

Virtue and vice are not terms that people are comfortable using. A lot of the people that I talk to say, "Oh, yeah, virtue and vices." I interviewed a number of college students, and they said, "Oh vice, yes, that's 'Miami Vice,' the TV program." Another person said, "Uhm, virtue. I just don't know what that means, I'm not a literate person." He meant he wasn't a literary person. He was a quite literate person.

The word "virtue" itself is seen largely by most Americans that I spoke with as an old-fashioned word with rather musty overtones. One person said that it reminded him of characters in a novel by Jane Austin. It was nice to discover that one of my respondents knew and read Jane Austin. Indeed, many of them knew that virtue was fashioned by some of the world's great moral philosophers and theologians who have written extensively on the subject.

One of the greatest theologians of the entire Christian tradition, Saint Augustine, said that honesty is a commandment, something that brings us in touch with God and his glory. He said that lying therefore is ungodly. Engaging in falsehood is always wrong. Lying, in other words, is something to be avoided at all costs. Honesty is a moral commandment, a moral absolute. It's a position grounded in religious thought, but not all that different from the great Enlightenment thinker, probably the greatest moral philosopher that ever lived, Immanuel Kant. He says very much the same thing, that it's always wrong to lie. Kant said that all moral commandments should be based on the idea of generalizing them as the universal law. If one person tells a lie and that is then universalized as a general law, with everyone following them, there will be no concept of truth in society whatsoever.

So it has been clearly recognized both by secular and religious thinkers that honesty is something that is at the heart of what it means to be virtuous. It is at the heart of what it is to be moral, and lying is always wrong.

I talked to 209 Americans in this study and I'd say that roughly 209 said that they could not live their lives that way. They respect honesty as a general idea. But when you explain what these great thinkers said, they respond that that's very nice but extremely idealistic and as a practical guideline for living, you cannot possibly do that. There are always circumstances in which it is justifiable to say something that is less than purely and perfectly honest.

So, what are we to conclude? Are we to conclude that people believe in the moral principle of lying all the time? No. But in a sense, people try to wrestle with how you can be faithful to the idea of honesty without necessarily always being honest under all circumstances.

What I try to report on when I write about the way people talk about honesty is some of the informal maxims or justifications that people develop about when it is right and proper and good and moral to be honest and when it might be justifiable not to be. For example, most people say that it is justifiable to be less than honest if doing so will avoid cruelty to others. In other words, there's one moral principle—be honest. And there's another moral principle—avoid cruelty. What happens if these two principles come into conflict?

Invariably people tell me that it is justified to be less than honest in order to avoid being cruel, and they could think of many circumstances in which that is necessary. In fact, some people said that the trouble they have with the person who is too honest is that there is a kind of sadistic quality to their honesty. They seem almost to want to be cruel to someone else. You don't go up to someone who is not dressed very well that day and say, "I've got to tell you, you look terrible." A moral person is not like that. There are always these kinds of judgments about honesty that you have to make. Furthermore, there may be degrees of honesty involved in many of these examples.

Similarly, people would generally agree that it is much more important to be honest to your friends than it is to be honest to people that you don't know as well. Indeed, it is much more important to be honest to a person than it is to be honest to an organization. People are very, very strongly convinced that organizations are inclined to do what they have to do to succeed and to get ahead. Thus, if you have to be dishonest, being dishonest to organizations is much more acceptable.

A few, not many, but a few people told me that they think it is okay to be dishonest to the Internal Revenue Service. Of 209 respondents, about five confessed to being dishonest to the IRS. I've done polling work which indicates the numbers are usually a little higher than that. But actually, we are a remarkably tax-compliant nation. Our tax system is almost entirely voluntary, especially in recent years, and it's amazing how many people pay what they consider to be their proper share (not necessarily every single cent that the government wants, but there is a kind of basic honesty there). Some people will say that the IRS is a kind of impersonal organization, and because it's impersonal, lying to that organization is on a morally different plane than lying to someone who's close to you.

But it wasn't just the IRS. I'm married to someone who is from another country, and in order to become an American citizen, she had to go through the process of naturalization with the Immigration and Naturalization Service. I can't tell you how many people think it is morally justified to lie to the Immigration and Naturalization Service, which has even a lower reputation in the United States, at least among people I talked to, than the Internal Revenue Service.

People also believe that it is justifiable to lie to someone if you think they are lying to you. This is a maxim with which both Kant and Augustine disagree entirely. In fact, Augustine would say that it is much more important to be honest to someone who is lying to you than it is to someone who is telling you the truth. If you lie to someone who is lying to you, you are putting yourself down on that person's level. But that is not the way most people think. If you feel that someone is apparently trying to take advantage of you, then that is an opportunity for you to be less than honest with them.

So there are many people who would say, "Wait a minute, the idea that you should always tell the truth is a wonderful principle but it is not the way that I can lead my life." Does that mean that we have lost the sense of virtue with respect to this particular principle?

Perhaps it can be argued either way. But I would point out that when Augustine made his strictures against lying, it did not take long before Saint Thomas Aquinas devoted a tremendous amount of theological reflection to cut away at the principle that honesty is always and only the best policy. By the time Aquinas was finished, there was not much left in terms of the injunction always to be honest.

Moreover, no sooner had Immanuel Kant published his work about honesty than another great philosopher, Benjamin Constant, said that it is justifiable to lie to someone who comes to your door asking if your wife is at home when he intends to kill your wife. The morally wrong thing to do under those circumstances would be to tell the truth.

So in fact, although I hesitate to use the term "situation ethics," this has been a very important approach in the Western intellectual tradition as well as absolutist ethics. And when Americans say that they want to be honest people but they cannot follow the commandment of being honest at all times, they have an intellectual justification behind it.

My role here is to present the evidence while other people draw the conclusions. If you believe that honesty is the only policy, you will find that Americans think about honesty in a hopelessly pragmatic way, hopelessly compromised, possibly immoral. But you can, at the same time, be impressed by the fact that people have not given up on the idea of honesty. They are trying to reconcile what they understand to be the enormous importance of being virtuous with the practical realities of what it means to live in a modern society in which case, it is rather remarkable that anything has survived under the rubric of honesty at all.

This is even more true of loyalty. Loyalty is another one of the great virtues in the Western tradition because loyalty is at the heart of the marriage vow that has played such an obvious and important role in our society. When we consider the divorce rates that have been presented to us, we would obviously conclude that there is a serious problem with loyalty. After all, when you get married, you take a pledge before God and before the state. To break that vow is a painful act of disloyalty. As Patrick Fagan has emphasized, it is a rejection about as painful an act as you can give to another person.

If Americans indeed feel very, very strongly that cruelty is something to be avoided, being disloyal can be phenomenally cruel. When we encounter these kinds of acts of disloyalty reflected in things like our divorce rate, or in the unwillingness of people to work for the same company for as long as they formerly did, or the people who join the Armed Forces not to serve their country but to get out as fast as they can so that they can get a college education or a better degree, or the athletes who spend three years with a team and then immediately try to get the highest bid that they can, or the owners of the teams that they work for who are also trying to move their franchise from one city to another no matter how much loyal support they have, these things send very, very powerful lessons indeed about loyalty.

Here again, we encounter a profound conflict when we talk to Americans about the importance of their belief in loyalty. They know how traitorous disloyalty always is yet, as they look around their society, they see that in fact it is basically the disloyal who are more often rewarded than the loyal. They see that the operating code in the labor market is to threaten to leave if you have the power to do so in order to get a better salary where you are. (In the academic world this has certainly become the order of the day.)

Many have experienced significant corporate downsizing, watching companies let employees go. One of the things I always try to find out when I interview people is to discover who their models are, who they cite, both as examples of good people and as examples of bad people. I cannot tell you how many Americans know that at the same time that the American Telephone and Telegraph Company laid off an extremely large number of their workers, the CEO of that company received a stock option that gave him an extraordinary amount. Those things stick in people's minds.

An amazing example to me, because I'm from Boston, was a man named Aaron Fuerstein who ran a company in Medford, Massachusetts, called Malden Mills in which there was a fire. He kept all of his employees on, even when the company wasn't producing anything, as an act of loyalty to them. That resonates with people. They may not remember his name, but they remember the incident. And one after another persons that I talk to will bring up an incident like that.

These messages are out there in the culture, and it becomes very, very clear that as important as loyalty has been, it has never been a virtue that in a free-enterprise economy has been all that valued. In fact, to start with, we speak of loyalty as a sort of feudalistic virtue that emphasizes that you should stay in one place, with one particular way of life, for your entire life. That comes directly into conflict with American values of mobility, of picking yourself up, of starting all over again. When I look at America, a land of opportunity with the highest rate at which people leave one community and move to another in the search of a better life, it is obvious that we are not a society that believes in loyalty of the "until death-do-us-part" variety.

I don't think in any way this excuses or explains away our high rates of divorce in the United States, which I personally find enormously troublesome. I think it is one of the single most serious social problems we have. Although the rates are evening out and flattening down, it is still one of the most serious challenges we face. I just do not think that it can be separated from the messages of disloyalty in the larger culture that resonate throughout the world of business, the world of sports, the world of entertainment, and elsewhere. These are the things people notice.

Self-discipline, the third of the four virtues that I talk to people about, is similar to what formerly was called the "Protestant ethic." It is the idea that you recognize the importance of restraining your impulses, of denying yourself pleasure in the short run for the sake of longer term obligations to others, and even for longer term obligations to yourself. You cannot be seduced by siren calls of hedonism. It is essential that you have a kind of stiff backbone and that you are able to resist temptation.

There are a number of images that, added together in many, many different forms, constitute a set of important ideas behind the virtue of self-restraint and self-discipline. These are values that Americans still pay an enormous amount of attention to when I talk to them. But interestingly enough, what a lot of people tell me is their justification for self-discipline is not to avoid the sins of self-indulgence but to better appreciate them. People say, "I understand that I give up this or that, but only so that I can binge somewhat later and enjoy it all that much more."

I ask people about themselves, "Do you think it is important to put limits on your own desires, to restrain your own appetites for example?" But then I also ask people about other people, "Do other people do a good job?" When people see self-indulgent people who cannot restrain themselves, they are unlike the classic Protestant ethic which would say, "Oh well, that person is dissolute, and that means that person is of a bad character." Instead they say, "That person is addicted to something." They medicalize their condition. They say people are driven by something over which they have no control. It is worlds away from the Protestant ethic. The Protestant ethic said not only that you should discipline yourself, but also that persons who do not discipline themselves are morally bad persons. Today people are not comfortable with that. They would much rather explain someone's bad habits as the product of a genetic or neurological condition over which they have no control, rather than Satan's work or some kind of deep character flaw. The language of addiction is enormously pervasive in American society. In a sense it has become our substitute for the Protestant ethic. It gives us a way of making sense out of our own behavior and out of the behavior of others.

I ask people a lot of questions about smoking in my surveys because I think it is an issue that gets people to talk about these things in a way that is very close to home. It is an issue that we all deal with. And if smoking is the example, then you could say, from the way people talked to me, that the American population is divided into two camps and two camps only.

In one camp are people who are addicted to smoking, and in the other camp are people who are allergic to smoking. It does not matter which one is which. They are both medicalized. In other words, if I smoke, it is not because I have a weakness of will. It is because I am addicted to smoking. I can't help it. And if I don't want you to smoke, I do not say, "Please don't smoke because smoking is morally wrong." I do not want to use the language of morality, so I say, "Please don't smoke because I'm allergic to it."

If I go up to another person and I say, "Would you please put out that cigarette because I think it is morally wrong for you to smoke," they will puff the smoke back into my face. But if I say, "Hey, I'm allergic to smoking," before you know it they're putting it out because we use the medical language on both sides of the debate much more than a moral language. So if we expect people to conduct themselves in the language of morality that is so much a part of the Western theological and moral tradition, we are likely to be disappointed.

Of all the four virtues, the one that fascinates me the most is forgiveness. Of all the virtues that I have been discussing, forgiveness is probably the most Christian in its character.

The origins of these other virtues are mainly Greek and Roman. The word virtue itself is a Roman word that comes from the Latin word *vir*, which actually has the same root as the word virility and means manliness. But we do not often think of forgiveness as a marshal or a military virtue. We think of it much more as a caring virtue, a virtue of empathy. And it is a virtue that is almost nonexistent in the Greek or Roman traditions.

It is, however, a virtue in the Jewish tradition. You do find in a number of the Old Testament stories themes of forgiveness. But I think it is fair to say that it is much more a virtue that is emphasized in the New Testament and that Jesus Christ is, of all the historical figures, the one who most embodies the virtue of forgiveness. So if you were to ask what is not necessarily the single most important Christian virtue, but almost the most essential Christian virtue, that might be forgiveness.

If you search William Bennett's book, *The Book of Virtues*, and look for forgiveness, you will not find it. *The Book of Virtues* is a big, thick book with a lot of stories in it. There are very few stories in the entire book from the New Testament. There are many more from Homer, like the *Iliad* and the *Odyssey*. Among the twelve chapters in *The Book of Virtues*, there is honor, there is loyalty, there is courage, and there is self-discipline. But forgiveness is not mentioned. In fact, forgiveness has almost completely disappeared even from many of the thinkers who write about how we've lost our sense of virtue.

The closest we have is compassion, which we associate with writers like Marvin Olasky. But when Marvin Olasky talks about compassion, much of the caring quality disappears. It becomes almost a stern compassion and loses much of what I think is the Christ-like quality that we generally associate with forgiveness.

So forgiveness is a very interesting virtue because it could almost be called the neglected virtue. Many of the people who write about virtues in the United States do not pay much attention to it.

What do Americans think about forgiveness? I think there would be a general sense that we are a very forgiving country. Certainly people who think that we have lost our stern moral character would probably consider that we are much too forgiving. And in some ways we are. The daytime television culture seems to say that no matter what you do, as long as you say, "I sinned and I ask for forgiveness," everybody will forgive you. There is a kind of willingness to forgive. I would not say Americans have forgiven Bill Clinton. They never did that. But I think that they wanted in some way to overlook what he had done. They did not share the view that what he had done was unforgivable in a legal sense.

But there is a very unforgiving side too. I did not tell you where I did my interviews. I did them all over the country, but twenty-five of them were done in and around a military base in San Antonio, Texas. Almost all of the people I talked to there were Hispanic Americans working on the military base. At the time that I was doing the interviews, the state of Texas executed Karla Fay Tucker. So the question of whether Karla Fay Tucker, who had discovered Christ in jail after having committed brutal murders, should be forgiven for her acts was a subject very much at the heart of these discussions. And almost all the people I talked to in San Antonio were Catholic.

As you know from the Pope's recent actions, forgiveness is at the heart of Catholic doctrine. It is absolutely essential to the nature of what it means to be Catholic. How many of the twenty-five people that I talked to in San Antonio wanted to forgive? Well, the general reaction was burn her. I should say that "fry her" was often the term used. It was not a very powerful idea with theological justification. Forgiveness is God's work, they would say, although Jesus does ask human beings to forgive one another as well. But they maintained, that's up to God and I am not going to get involved in that one. I guess that is why we have a God because he can make those decisions, and people do not feel comfortable making them.

So if one is looking for a sense of the vibrant, deep, moral discourse to resonate among ordinary Americans in the great tradition of Western moral thinking, incorporating all the right theological insights and religious traditions that have shaped America, one is going to be disappointed. It does not resonate at the level of what Americans say.

Yet I am persuaded that the moral condition of Americans is not nearly as bad as some of the diagnoses would lead us to believe. What I see is people who are saying that the virtues are enormously important to them, but they also recognize that they are a free people. They are a people that have the great blessing of a fantastic amount of economic freedom. They also have an extraordinary amount of political freedom. They can vote for whomever they want. They elect their own leaders. How many people in the world can say that they are blessed with the political freedom that Americans have?

It seems to me that a country composed of people who can buy whatever they want and go wherever they choose are not going to say, when it comes to morality, that they must obey orders given to them from someone else. They are going to say that they want the same kind of freedom over their moral lives that they have in their economic lives and in their political lives.

This does not mean they are going to be immoral with their freedom. I find most Americans to be morally decent. They are a generous and good people. But they are asking, "How can you tell us that we are free in all these other areas and then say that when it comes to the truly deep things, to the really profound things, to the things that make us who we are, that as a people we do not have a say over the rules that are going to govern the morality by which we are expected to live?" People want that kind of freedom also.

A good deal of what the diagnosticians of America's moral state have been finding is a certain discomfort with that kind of freedom. There is a certain feeling that people are not living by the old moral rules anymore, and indeed they are not. The country has been dramatically changed over the last thirty or forty years. But I do not believe that it is about to collapse. I do not believe that it is about to fall apart. I am a tremendous optimist about the United States.

What I think we are witnessing is a period of adjustment in which the idea that people are in charge of their own destinies—a feeling that has been so much at the heart of the American experience—should apply to morality just as it is applied to economics and politics. If it is abused, of course, it becomes pure, reckless hedonism. If it becomes a culture of "me firstism," then moral freedom will be fantastically abused just as economic freedom and political freedom can be abused. But if used responsibly and if it is used well, it will give people a stronger morality than any we have had before because they will invest in their own morality. They will consider it their own and it is likely to be much more powerful than any we have ever had.

As demonstrated by Pat Fagan's diagrams, we are beginning to see an upturn in the last few years. The real rates have declined in all of these categories and have now begun to turn around. As anyone who lives in New York City can attest, the crime rate has fallen dramatically. When Bill Bennett publishes his surveys of the leading indicators of moral health, they are all turning around.

We don't know, of course, whether that will continue. They could slip. They could have a correction like the Nasdaq. But the optimism in me tells me that we have hit the bottom and that what we are now witnessing is the upturn that is inevitable when people discover that they can have a role in the way they live and, with truth, can exercise it carefully and responsibly.

Chapter 13

The Moral Roots of American Society

Steve Forbes

What is the moral basis of a free society? In the aftermath of the Cold War, that question is a top priority. Is there cause for optimism that the severe cultural crisis we've been experiencing for the last thirty or forty years—an explosion in teen pregnancy, violent crime, illegal drug use, divorce, spiritual apathy—can be turned around?

Can our social wounds be healed? What role, if any, does government have in assisting moral and spiritual renewal here at home and in providing for bold moral leadership around the globe?

These are important questions for leaders and citizens of a democracy, especially for the world's only superpower. Yet too many in our political class and intellectual class ignore such questions. When you bring up religion, when you bring up morality, there seems to be some feeling in these circles that supposedly sophisticated people just do not discuss such concerns.

The reason there is resistance to the moral and spiritual issues of life among our elites is because many are uncomfortable discussing the seeming intangibles of life. Such fear causes them to seek the seemingly solid ground of poll results, leading economic indicators, and the like, which shows they are of sound mind, not getting into this kind of soft stuff. Thus, they have trouble conversing about the things that matter most. And you can see what has happened to religion in the last three decades. In America it has been trivialized and marginalized. For years it has been treated as something almost like a hobby. Some are interested in anthropology, some in sociology, and some in religion. To the sophisticate's mind, this is all right because it's a free country. But it's something you keep at home. You do not discuss it outside the home.

As the twentieth century came to an end, the world concluded from America's experience that the economic and political freedoms that come from capitalism and democracy are truly the most powerful and productive ways to organize society. At the same time, however, we in America have been realizing

135

that if you want a healthy, vibrant society, capitalism and democracy alone are not enough.

Now that statement may seem a bit surprising coming from the CEO of the nation's leading capitalist magazine, whose motto is "Capitalist tool." But it is true. Capitalism and democracy are necessary but insufficient elements of a successful, virtuous, and vibrant society. A free society depends upon much more than free elections and free markets. A self-governing society must be made up of self-governing individuals, individuals with a moral sense and a moral compass, a set of fixed principles that guide and direct them regardless of the fads, whims, and predilections of the day.

Ronald Reagan made this point consistently. A free society requires a moral foundation. A breakdown of the moral foundation of society has severe consequences. He was absolutely right. Clearly the bitter lesson of the last thirty or forty years is that an explosion of social pathologies undermines the blessings of liberty and prosperity.

The stakes, therefore, are enormous. Not only do we have responsibilities for future generations of Americans, we have a responsibility to current generations all around the globe. If America gets things right, politically and morally, then the rest of the world has a chance to get these things right. But if America gets into trouble, then truly, the rest of the world is in trouble. In that sense, we are the only hope left—the only superpower in the world.

So what, then, is freedom? When the government of China, for example, tells people they can read state-run newspapers but cannot print and distribute Bibles, and imprisons and tortures dissidents, which it still does, or tells people that you can have one child but not two, forcing many women to have unwanted abortions, or that people can watch state-run television but not listen to Radio Free Asia, that is not freedom. The absence of centralized state control, however, is not necessarily freedom either. Just look at Beirut. The people there are not free. Neither are the people of Cartagena, the drug capital of Colombia. Freedom is not anarchy; it is not chaos; it is not mayhem; and it is not what the great liberal, classic economist Ludwig von Mises condemned as the freedom to let false forces operate. That is simply tyranny in another guise.

Americans have always defined true freedom as an environment in which one may resist evil and do what is right, noble, and good and do it without fear of reprisal. It is the presence of justice and mercy. It is where the rule of law is based on fundamentals and nonnegotiable moral truths that are simple and easy to understand and are fairly and effectively administered. It offers individuals and families equal opportunity to better their lives morally, spiritually, intellectually, and economically. Freedom is not a commodity for dictators to distribute and deny at will. Nor is it a moral, spiritual, or political vacuum in which anything goes, as too often has happened in recent times.

Freedom is a priceless treasure that the state is supposed to safeguard and defend, because human beings have an intrinsic right to be free. And that right comes not from the state, but from God.

To the Founding Fathers, this was a self-evident truth. It is fundamental to the American experiment. The founders believed that man's place in the universe was no accident. They believed that man and the world in which he lives were created and sustained by a just and living God. George Washington said it very well. He said: "It is impossible to jump to a creation of the universe without the agency of a Supreme Being. It is impossible to govern the universe without the aid of a Supreme Being."[1] James Madison, the father of our Constitution, said, "The belief in a God all-powerful, wise, and good is so essential to the moral order of the world and to the happiness of man that arguments which enforce it cannot be drawn from too many sources."[2]

Now this assurance of God's presence and divine guidance has been under siege in our culture for much of the twentieth century. The founders of this country staked the country's future on the principle that human beings are created by God and that, therefore, they have certain intrinsic, nonnegotiable, absolute rights. "All men are created equal," reads the Declaration of Independence, "and are endowed by their Creator with certain inalienable rights. That among these are life, liberty, and the pursuit of happiness." Government's role in society, then, is to secure these rights, not to create or dispense them. This is the moral basis of a free society.

Now the order of these rights, first life, then freedom, then the equal opportunity to pursue one's own happiness, was written with great care and precision. Remember that order: life, liberty, and the pursuit of happiness. The founders understood the need to balance man's right to be free with man's responsibility to life. A person's right to life supersedes another's freedom to rob banks and to kill people. Again, the ordering of man's rights may seem simple and obvious, but it is the linchpin of Western civilization. Switch the order, putting happiness before liberty, or liberty before life, and you end up with moral squalor. Deny the God-given nature of these rights and you open the door to tyranny.

Thomas Jefferson asked: "Can the liberties of a nation be sure when we remove their only firm basis—a conviction in the minds of the people that these liberties are the gift of God?"[3] John Adams put it this way:

> We have no government armed with power capable of containing the human passions unbridled by morality and religion. Avarice, ambition, revenge, or gallantry would break the strongest cords of our Constitution as water goes through a net. Our Constitution was made only for a moral and religious people. It is wholly inadequate to the government of any other.[4]

The people of the former Soviet Union are finding this out the hard way in the tragic drama that my colleagues and I at *Forbes* magazine have been writing about. Communism destroyed not only material objects, it destroyed the moral and spiritual foundations of that country as well. The people of the former Soviet Union are discovering that without a moral foundation, it is nearly impossible to have a self-governing free society. Theft is rampant. The murder rate is almost seven times our own. Mafias are moving into the vacuum left after the collapse of communism to seize vast sectors of the economic activity in that former empire. A Hobbesian world has emerged there in too many parts of the former Soviet Union, where life indeed is nasty, brutish, and short. It is no coincidence that the longevity of the Russian male today is now late fifties.

Sadly, today in America, many of the basic moral truths spoken of in the Constitution are, apparently, not so self-evident to everyone. The statistics for the last forty years are grim, but the anecdotal evidence truly hits home. Like the story of the eighteen-year-old New Jersey girl attending her senior prom who allegedly delivered her baby in a restroom, left the newborn in a plastic bag in a trash can—where it suffocated to death—cleaned herself up, went back to the dance floor, and requested that the DJ play a favorite song. In a culture where an American president vetoes a ban on partial-birth abortions, how are we supposed to teach children the inherent value of human life? Is what happened in Jonesboro, Arkansas, simply an aberration, or is it part of a pattern of a culture we have allowed to arise in the last three decades?

Of course, there has always been crime in America. There has been crime since the creation of man. But in America, we have not always been so uncertain, so confused about what is right and what is wrong, what is acceptable and what is to be forcefully condemned. And that must be clear. A free society cannot survive the collapse of the two-parent family. It cannot survive children growing up without a father's love and discipline. It cannot survive an explosion in violent crime. Nor can it survive a generation of crack babies and teenagers whose minds and bodies are being destroyed by illegal drugs.

Like millions of Americans, my wife and I are deeply concerned about the moral conditions of our nation. We have been raising five daughters in a society where, at times, it seems the wheels are coming off. It is difficult enough in any era to raise young girls to become wise and virtuous young women. But raising young women today is particularly tough. You've seen it—movies, TV, music, and the Internet bombard young people today with messages of sexual revolution in the materialistic, self-absorbed culture that tempts them away from good moral character. This culture has not appealed to the "better angels of our nature." And affluence does not protect children from temptation. In fact, sometimes, it makes temptation more accessible.

The good news, though, is that there is hope. This is not the first time in America when we have faced such difficult times and then turned things around. We have had several periods of exciting renewal in our history, most notably, the Second Great Awakening in the early 1800s and later the Progressive Era at the turn of the twentieth century. Consider the state of America in the 1820s. We think we have substance abuse problems today. In the 1820s alcohol consumption in America was about five times per person what it is today. Everybody in those days seemed to be taking it straight from the jug. They called it hard cider, but it had nothing to do with what you buy at the supermarket today. This was the real stuff, and everyone drank it. Teachers, preachers, even kids, if they went to school, wanted it from the jug as well. So by noontime, much of the nation was in a kind of haze.

While we chuckle about it today, this rampant alcoholism had all the predictable social consequences. So there arose a series of movements in America to galvanize those words that were mentioned in the beginning—that a self-governing nation must be inhabited by self-governing individuals. Consequently, the first public health movement in America did not come out of Washington, D.C. It was the Temperance Movement, and it worked. Within a generation, alcohol consumption fell by more than half. The era also saw the rise of a series of religious movements, known to historians as the Second Great Awakening. The same period also saw the rise of the Abolition Movement against slavery.

On the political side, in the early twentieth century, Teddy Roosevelt had come to personify reform. He came to power during a troubled time, when people felt America had lost its way as it tried to make the transition from an agricultural society to an industrial society. But Roosevelt had hardly taken the oath of office after McKinley's assassination before he was busting up trusts and monopolies, championing the right of women to vote, and attacking political corruption in Washington. He believed that government did have a vital role to play. He also coined the term "bully pulpit." He used the presidency to publicly, vigorously, and consistently reassert the notion that there must be a moral foundation to a free society. He urged people to take their faith seriously. He knew that there is a limit to what government can do. TR's methods worked. The national anxiety of the 1890s was replaced with a sense of confidence about the future.

This gets to one of the great strengths of American democracy. It is not that we do not make mistakes; we are human. But when we do stumble or fall, we not only pick ourselves up but, looking to God and working with others, we find the inner strength to reach new heights. We have done it before, and it looks like America is beginning to do it again. That is why I believe there is reason for optimism. The end of the Cold War means we can downsize Washington and return power and control to families and communities. Right now in Washington, it seems that politicians have been led astray. But that may be, and should be, only a detour.

The dawn of the Information Age has given individuals more choice and control over their daily lives, and there are encouraging signs that we are entering a new season of moral and spiritual renewal. We saw this in the welfare debate in 1996. For once it was not about money; it was about the old system hurting and destroying the very people it was supposed to help. We see it in ministries working in the inner city. Efforts in certain areas that have not received much national publicity are starting to have a real impact on young people. We see it in the surges of baby-boomers who are going back to church and to temple. Some are returning for their own spiritual needs and some to build strong moral foundations within their children.

We are seeing this renewal in the growing movement of inner-city schools that are educating kids for college and real careers. Last summer I visited the family of Pat and Lee Holland. Economic poverty? Absolutely. Their family academy is right in the center of Harlem. A block away you see the drug dealers at work. But moral and spiritual poverty? Not a chance at this school. Here were teachers pouring their hearts and souls into kids, and the kids were responding, learning, graduating, and making lives for themselves. Why? Because of bureaucrats in the Department of Education or at the National Education Association's crystal palace in Washington, D.C.? No. Because some unsung American heroes are taking matters into their own hands—and succeeding.

You saw this also with the Promise Keepers who marched on Washington. Think about that for a moment. First, hundreds of thousands of virile men, going to a big city for a weekend and behaving themselves. And, even more remarkably, going to Washington, D.C., and not asking for anything. They were simply promising that they would meet their responsibilities to their families and their communities. There is today, I think, a sense that people are increasingly in agreement with Will Rogers' wonderful advice on family values. He said people should conduct themselves at home so that they would not be ashamed to sell the family parrot to the town gossip.

The question is: What is government's role? Samuel Johnson put it in perspective. He said, "How small of all that human hearts endure, that part which laws or kings can cause or cure!"[5] Government cannot transform lives, nor can it instill lasting moral virtues within our children. But government does have a limited and specific role to play in reasserting a moral foundation, a moral basis for a free society.

Let me mention a few ways government can reassert this moral basis. Government, for instance, must appoint judges and Supreme Court justices who understand the moral and ethical principles upon which this nation is founded. We can reinforce the importance of the marriage contract. We can overhaul and simplify the tax code to allow struggling families to keep more of what they earn. We can reform adoption laws. We can reject preferential policies so that Americans can begin life as individuals and not as members of groups, as we see in the Balkans. We can fight an effective, relentless war against illegal drugs. And we can also override the president's veto of the bill banning partial-birth abortions which, as you well know, is a particularly gruesome form of infanticide.

This is a sensitive area. But if we approach it in the manner of a conversation rather than by screeching, if we approach it in a manner of persuasion, this can be an issue that does not just divide the nation as it has in the past. Rather, it can unite and inspire the nation. It is based on a basic principle of American law, simply, that the law protects not just the strong, the healthy, and the rich. The law protects all of us, including the weak, including the elderly, the infirm, and the unborn. An individual's right to life is not a government-endowed right. It is a Creator-endowed right. And this is where we need a national conversation to find our bearings again.

I believe in life. And I also believe that there have been great transformations in the past in American history. We can have a great transformation again. I believe, and I hope that more people will come to believe, that life truly begins at conception and ends, and should end, only at natural death. Each of these policies in its own way reaffirms the moral basis of a free society. Each is rooted in the religious principles that undergird Western civilization.

Now let me address another thing that government can do, and that is to help halt worldwide religious persecution. Remarkably, one of the most under-reported stories of our time is the growing persecution of Christian, Buddhist, Moslem, Hindu, Jewish, and other religious minorities around the world. There are arbitrary arrests, beatings, burnings, crucifixions, and other horrifying forms of torture. Executions are occurring in such nations as China, Vietnam, Iran, and Pakistan. In the Sudan, the Islamic fundamentalist government there has literally slaughtered tens of thousands of Christians who live predominantly in that country's southern region. Indeed, what has happened in southern Sudan is no less than genocide. We must never again make the mistake that we made during World War II, when we knew the Holocaust was underway, with mass massacres in Eastern Europe, and we said nothing and did nothing.

We must also speak out against all human rights abuses. We must particularly be outspoken about China's abuses, whether it's slave labor camps, forced sterilization, forced abortions, executing prisoners to obtain body parts to sell, maintaining death-factory orphanages (as the *New York Times* wrote about a little over a year ago), or imprisoning Christian pastors and priests. That is what the "bully pulpit" is there for. The president can use it. Yet, unfortunately, our recent president and vice president were silent on these atrocities. President Clinton labeled his China policy "constructive engagement," but "indifferent and incomplete" would have been be more accurate.

America is the world's only superpower and should do more. We should recognize that while we must have open commerce with the world, hoping that forces will arise to help bring about liberal reforms in these countries, America still has a unique role, because of our singular origins, to highlight abuses, with the hope that reform will follow. We should do more Radio Free Asia broadcasting. Radio Free Europe worked in Central Europe and the former Soviet Union, and that type of broadcasting can work in other dark places in the world. We should increase funding for the National Endowment for Democracy. The free flow of trade is deadly to dictatorial regimes, and we should be ready to impose sanctions on military-owned companies in China. The Chinese are very sensitive to international activity, and we should use that to our advantage. Specifically, Congress is considering the Freedom from Religious Persecution Act, sponsored by Congressman Frank R. Wolf of Virginia and Senator Arlen Spector of Pennsylvania. It is a move in the right direction, particularly if its language on trade is targeted to products used in torture and violence. And with these concrete items, the Wolf-Spector bill reasserts the principle that government's essential role is to protect life and liberty, not to subsidize terror and intimidation.

As Alexis de Toqueville noted so eloquently 160 years ago, America has never been a top-down nation. Our moral and creative energies come from within. We have always built our nation from the ground up. That is the great historic strength of America. Now, I believe we are at the beginning of a fourth Great Awakening, and none too soon.

From the beginning of our nation's history, Americans have understood that freedom has three vital components: economic, political, and moral. In the twentieth century, the arguments for economic and political freedom have been won. Now the battle is on the moral front, to establish in our minds a strong sense of what is right and what is wrong. Technology, in and of itself, is too often value-free. After all, fire gives us warmth; but fire also gave us Auschwitz. Relearning the truth that a moral basis must undergird a free society is one of the great unfinished challenges of our time. We must teach our children, both to remind them and to communicate to others, that man's right to live free, to pursue happiness, to own property comes from God and is to be secured by the state. We must assert vigorously, here at home and overseas, the fundamental importance of faith and religious liberty in sustaining both democracy and freedom.

America has the potential for the greatest economic boom and spiritual renewal in its history. As we have done numerous times in our past, we can once again expand opportunities for everyone, reform our corrupt political institutions, and renew and restore the severely weakened moral foundation of our country. In so doing, we can truly fulfill our national destiny as the leader of the free world.

Can we make these glaring opportunities come to pass? Can we rise to the occasion? Or will we be known to future generations as the era of missed opportunities? That is the great question of our time. I am an optimist. I believe that we are approaching an era which will prove, once again, that the American people rose to the occasion. Future historians will conclude that we proved the critics and the skeptics wrong. That the American nation, once again, resumed its rightful place as the leader and inspiration of the world.

Notes

1. Tim LaHaye, *Faith of Our Founding Fathers*, (Master Books, 1996), 104.

2. LaHaye, *Faith of our Founding Fathers*, 131.

3. Thomas Jefferson, *Notes on the State of Virginia*, ed. William Peden (Chapel Hill, N.C.: University of North Carolina Press, 1955), 163.

4. *The Works of John Adams*, Vol. 19, ed. C. F. Adams (New York: AMS Press Inc., 1971), 239.

5. John Bartlett, *Familiar Quotations*, 10th ed. (Boston, Mass.: Little Brown, 1919), #4007, see: www.bartleby.com/100/249.24.html (22 Aug. 2001) from Samuel Johnson, *Goldsmith's Traveler* (New York: Bartleby.com, 2000).

Chapter 14

My Faith and I

William E. Simon Sr.

Early Tenets of Faith

Elsewhere in this volume, two brilliant people—Jim Wilson and John DiIulio—wrote about the importance of religious values in our society—about the difference faith makes when it comes to motivating people to change their lives and of the now irrefutable evidence that religion is a vital factor in reducing crime, welfare dependence, divorce, and other social ills.

Of course, religion can be a very delicate subject and one that is difficult to speak about in a personal way. Faith has always been very much a given in my life. I am a Christian, a practicing, life-long member of the Roman Catholic church. And, while I've never been one who wears his religion on his sleeve, I believe wholeheartedly in the basic tenets of our faith.

These principles were taught to me in a loving and compelling way, first by my family, and then by the dedicated nuns in the Catholic schools I attended as a boy. My parents were a wonderful example of the Catholic faith. I remember, like yesterday, attending Mass with my family every Sunday. I served as an altar boy at the seven o'clock Mass several days a week during the summer before going out to caddy or to work on the beach.

Over the years, there have certainly been periods of greater and lesser religious devotion in my life, and my participation in religious activities has ebbed and flowed. I confess that, for too many years after our family was well launched, my life was defined and guided far less by my church and its teachings than by practical pursuits.

143

Years of Neglect

I was young, had a lot of drive and confidence, and enjoyed a great deal of success at an early age. I was fortunate to arrive on Wall Street in the early 1950s when the post-war economic boom created abundant opportunities for young men with ambition and an appetite for hard work. Like many of my friends and colleagues, I enjoyed great success on Wall Street during the 1950s, 1960s, and early 1970s, and I eventually became a senior partner at Salomon Brothers and a member of the executive committee.

In 1972, shortly after the November elections, President Nixon asked me to join his administration. Over the next four years, I served in both the Nixon and Ford administrations as deputy secretary of the treasury, head of the Federal Energy Office, and, finally, as secretary of the treasury. I became aware not only of the benefits, but also the burdens of high office. They were exciting and, indeed, tragic times. During that period, I often felt like I was in an endless race requiring the speed of a sprinter and the endurance of a marathoner. Every day seemed to bring a new challenge or, indeed, a new crisis.

I did not realize it at the time, but I now see that I was in neglect in those years. I neglected not only my family, but also my religion.

The philosopher G. K. Chesterton once observed that Christianity has not been tried and found wanting, but rather it has been found difficult and thus too often left untried.[1] Unfortunately, those penetrating words have too often had a ring of truth in my life. That is why I have never hesitated to recognize that I am really a failed and flawed mortal, so I always approach the subject of religion and my personal faith with an abundance of humility and with a certain degree of self-consciousness.

The Role of Religion

Before I elaborate on my own charitable activities, let me just say a few words about the subject of this conference—the role of religion in public life—and, I would add, in private life as well.

When I listen to scholars like Jim Wilson and John DiIulio, I become hopeful that our citizens and leaders are coming to understand that religious values must play a greater role in our debates over such issues as crime, drugs, welfare, broken families, and, yes, education.

Beginning three or four decades ago, our country embarked on a tragic experiment in which we tried to strip religious principles out of public life—out of our schools, out of public programs to help the needy, and out of our public debates. Well, we have seen the results of this misguided experiment in the statistics on crime, welfare, divorce, and drug use that are so familiar to us all.

Government Roadblocks

In recent years, in my charitable work with the sick, the poor, and the forgotten, I have come to understand in a personal and practical way that faith-based ministries can accomplish much more than any government program ever can. Still, government bureaucrats continue to do all they can to keep these ministries out of public programs and institutions.

For example, a few years ago Teen Challenge, a faith-based drug treatment program in San Antonio, was enjoying great success in getting addicts off drugs. In fact, it had a far higher success rate than any government treatment program and at far less cost. And how did the state of Texas respond to this dramatic success story? To no one's surprise, the state Texas tried to shut the program down. Why? Well, because the counselors were not licensed.[2]

Consider another example. For many years volunteers with Prison Fellowship Ministries have gone into America's prisons to minister to inmates. Led by Chuck Colson, Prison Fellowship's goal is to break the cycle of crime by changing the hearts and minds of people convicted of crimes.

And it works. Recidivism refers to the percentage of inmates who return to a life of crime upon their release from prison. This, indeed, is the true measure of how effective incarceration programs are. As we know, the rate of recidivism is very high in America's prisons. In state prisons across the country, the rate of recidivism is an astonishing 93 percent. Obviously, our present methods of incarceration are not doing a good job of rehabilitating inmates and of turning them into productive citizens. Indeed, in many places, our prisons are doing just the opposite—they are turning many prisoners into hardened criminals who can never be safely returned to society.

But it is a different story when it comes to inmates who take part in Prison Fellowship programs. Prison Fellowship believes that crime is a moral problem that requires a moral solution. In other words, you have to change a prisoner's heart before you can change his behavior.

We now have solid evidence that this approach works. The Center for Social Research has just done a study that showed that when prisoners attended at least ten Prison Fellowship Bible studies, only 14 percent were rearrested within a year following their release.[3] Fourteen percent versus 93 percent: It is an astounding difference.

Despite these successes, Prison Fellowship still faces many roadblocks when it tries to go into prisons across the country. A few years ago, prison officials refused to allow Prison Fellowship to come in and minister to inmates at the Maryland State Penitentiary. In all fifty states, Prison Fellowship employees have to spend up to a quarter of their time just trying to deal with bureaucratic requirements.

But, when it comes to hostility to religion, these examples represent only the tip of the iceberg.

Freedom of Religion?

Each December, the American Civil Liberties Union (a misnomer if I ever heard one) launches its annual attack on Nativity scenes and other Christmas displays that towns and cities erect in their parks and public squares. According to the ACLU's ridiculous reasoning, placing a crèche or a menorah on public property represents an establishment of religion. Sadly, our courts have frequently sided with this outrageous argument. Who are these lunatics who can persuade the Supreme Court and our cultural elite that it is against the law to celebrate the birth of Jesus Christ? Our country was founded by people fleeing persecution. They wanted to enjoy the blessings of freedom—freedom of speech, freedom of press, freedom of assembly, and, yes, freedom of religion.

But nowhere, I suppose, is religion less welcome than in our public schools. For decades now we have been hearing the chant that religion does not belong in public life—whatever that means. Probably the most influential voice on this subject has been the United States Supreme Court which, in 1962, made its absurd and astonishing decision to forbid the saying of prayers in public schools— a decision that flies in the face of our history and heritage, our Constitution, and the intentions of our Founding Fathers.

As I have said, America was settled by people of various faiths fleeing religious persecution. They came to America to find a place where they could practice their religion openly, without fear of persecution and retaliation. For more than three-hundred years after the Pilgrims stepped foot on Plymouth Rock, our heritage and our institutions were built on a firm belief in God. Our history is replete with examples of our religious commitment. Our Constitution guarantees freedom of religion—one of the few freedoms that is explicitly mentioned in our Constitution.

Yes, our Constitution guarantees the free exercise of religion. But this freedom has been stripped away by judges who have discarded the rights of the 90 percent of Americans who believe in God in favor of the 10 percent who do not. I find it impossible to understand how we can tolerate a decision that so plainly restricts the practice of religion.

What has happened in our country was summed up beautifully in a beseeching little poem—one might call it a prayer—that was allegedly written by a young grammar school student in a public school:

> Now I sit me down in school,
> Where praying is against the rule.
> For this great nation under God
> Finds public mention of him odd.
> Any prayer a class recites
> Now violates the Bill of Rights.
> Any time my head I bow
> Becomes a federal matter now.
> Teach us of stars or pole or equator
> But make no mention of their creator.

In silence alone we can meditate
And if God can be reached,
Well, that is great.
This rule, however, has one gimmick in it;
You have to be finished
In less than a minute.
If not, O lord, this one plea I make:
Should I be knifed in school
My soul you'll take.[4]

Of course, this is not how our laws were interpreted during America's first 186 years. It was not until that disgraceful school prayer decision in 1962 that the courts began to build a steep wall between religion and public life.

Our Founders' Intent

This is not what our founders intended. They meant the link between religion and public life to be strong and healthy. In fact, our founders were convinced that self-government was not possible without religious faith. As John Adams put it, "Our Constitution was made ONLY for a moral and religious people. It is wholly inadequate to the government of any other."[5]

George Washington in his farewell address reminded Americans that "of all the habits which lead to political prosperity, religion and morality are indispensable supports. They are the firmest props for the duties of men and citizens."[6]

And the founders did not expect Americans to be religious merely in the privacy of their homes. Their purpose was to weave these principles of religious faith in and around the institutions by which we order our lives. They intended for schools and civic associations to have a religious air, permeated by the values that created and shaped our culture. They recognized that only God can give us the wisdom that is needed to guide the affairs of a great nation.

At a particularly contentious moment during the Constitutional Convention in 1787, Benjamin Franklin took the floor and observed: "I have lived, Sir, a long time, and the longer I live, the more convincing proofs I see of this truth—that God governs the affairs of men. And if a sparrow cannot fall to the ground without God's notice, is it probable that an empire can rise without His aid?" Franklin proceeded to introduce the following motion—"that henceforth prayers imploring the assistance of Heaven, and its blessings on our deliberations, be held in this Assembly every morning before we proceed to business, and that one or more of the Clergy of this city be requested to officiate in this service."[7] His motion was introduced in an assembly that included such men as Washington, James Madison, Alexander Hamilton, Robert Morris, and other illustrious members who went on to become leaders of the new republic.

Even Thomas Jefferson, not noted for his religious zeal, authorized the use of public funds to support missionaries to the Indians in the Northwest Territories.

This religious example set by our Founding Fathers was followed by other leaders in subsequent periods in our history.

Abraham Lincoln, in particular, frequently called on the aid of God to see the nation through the great crisis of the Civil War. In early 1863, at a time when the war was going badly for Union forces, Lincoln issued a proclamation calling for a national day of fasting and prayer. His proclamation begins with these words:

> Whereas it is the duty of nations as well as of men to own their dependence upon the overruling power to God, to confess their sins and transgressions in humble sorrow, yet with assured hope that genuine repentance will lead to mercy and pardon; and to recognize the sublime truth, announced in the Holy Scriptures and proven by all history, that those nations only are blessed whose God is the Lord."[8]

Why was it necessary to call for a national day of fasting and prayer? Lincoln's answer has meaning for us today: "We have been the recipients of the choicest bounties of heaven," he wrote.

> We have been preserved these many years in peace and prosperity. We have grown in numbers, wealth, and power. But we have forgotten God. We have forgotten the gracious hand which preserved us in peace, and multiplied and enriched and strengthened us; and we have vainly imagined, in the deceitfulness of our hearts, that all these blessings were produced by some superior wisdom and virtue of our own.[9]

So Lincoln called on the nation to acknowledge its dependence on God and to ask for his aid through the crisis of war.

Lincoln probably invoked God's assistance more than any of our presidents. His magnificent Second Inaugural Address, given just six weeks before he was assassinated and as the war was nearing an end, is filled with religious images from both the Old and the New Testaments. Who can ever forget the inspiring words he used to end this address:

> With malice toward none, with charity for all. With firmness in the right, *as God gives us to see the right*, let us strive on to finish the work we are in: to bind up the nation's wounds, to care for him who shall have borne the battle, and for his widow and his orphan—to do all which may achieve and cherish a just and lasting peace among ourselves, and with all nations.[10]

Was Lincoln wrong to remind the nation of its reliance on God and to invoke his assistance during those perilous times? Well, according to our contemporary Supreme Court and to a great many of our so-called intellectual and cultural leaders, Lincoln was misguided in these appeals. But, of course, it was Lincoln who was right and our present elites who are wrong.

In God We Trust

Alexis de Tocqueville approvingly described this infusion of faith into our public life as America's "biblical fragrance." That biblical fragrance has wafted throughout most of our history and is reflected in countless ways in our institutions. Our currency is emblazoned with the bold statement, "In God We Trust." (I should know, because I signed the currency when I was Secretary of the Treasury.) Our Pledge of Allegiance contains the apt phrase "one nation, under God." And Congress begins its sessions with a prayer, just like our Founding Fathers.

And there is much more. Two hundred years ago, churches set up societies to help destitute widows and orphans. One hundred and fifty years ago, people of faith led the Abolitionist Movement to rid America of slavery. One hundred years ago, people inspired by religion put an end to child labor in the factories of New England.

Seventy years ago, Dorothy Day began the Catholic Worker Movement in New York City, weaving the love of God around the sick, hungry, and destitute. Forty years ago, people of faith, most especially the Reverend Martin Luther King Jr., led the Civil Rights Movement.

It is no accident that many of our hospitals have names like St. Mary's, Sacred Heart, St. Luke's, Beth Israel, and Mt. Sinai. After all, they were built by people with a strong faith in God.

Our churches and synagogues once performed many of the tasks that government has taken over—taking care of the widow and orphan, feeding the hungry, and reaching out to unwed mothers. But, early in this century, we began to accept the idea that "Big Brother" can do a better job than God of assisting people in need.

Today, we have ample evidence of how wrong this belief is. In many cases, government meddling has made the plight of the poor even worse. Sadly, that biblical fragrance that Tocqueville celebrated has been greatly weakened—in part because our cultural elites and bureaucrats raise a stink whenever believers seek to enter the public arena to help the sick, the poor, the prisoner, or the drug addict—and because government bureaucrats have thrown up so many roadblocks that faith-based ministries find it difficult to do their jobs.

I am presently trying to buy two condemned buildings in New York City so that Mother Teresa's Missionaries of Charity can establish a shelter for the homeless and destitute. These buildings are abandoned. They have been off the city's tax rolls for years. The project itself will not cost the city a dime—but bureaucrats in the city government have managed to tie the project up for two years with countless legal technicalities. Because of their resistance, I am not sure if this shelter will ever be built—which would be a tragic shame for the poor and homeless in New York City.

This is a perfect example of the bureaucratic approach to compassion. They care more about their own turf and their regulations than about genuine acts of mercy, and they will do anything to keep faith-based ministries from showing what they can accomplish.

Let's face it, government cannot do this job as well as our churches, synagogues, and faith-based ministries. Why? Because the people who run government programs see their work as nothing but a job. They have all the passion for the poor as a fax machine. But faith-based charities are run by people who are living out God's command to serve "the least of these" with all their hearts and minds and souls.

My Journey of Faith

As I come down the home stretch of my time here on earth, I cannot help but reflect on how deeply, and for whatever reason, God has blessed me in my life. I have prospered in the world of business and finance. I have had the high honor of serving my country. I have traveled the globe and sat with presidents, prime ministers, and kings.

And, of course, I have received many honors among men. While I appreciate these incredible adventures and experiences, I can truthfully tell you that nothing I have done, no honor I have received, no amount of wealth I have accumulated has brought me as much satisfaction as my charitable work with the sick, the poor, and the forgotten.

I have learned that as we live out God's command to reach out to the needy, we discover something surprising. The person who benefits most is not the one being served, but the one doing the serving. I would like to share why this is so.

One of the first experiences that helped me on my journey to become a better Catholic and Christian was becoming involved with Covenant House in New York. This is an organization that houses and protects runaway youth, many of whom are addicted to alcohol and drugs or afflicted with disease. It was started thirty years ago by a Franciscan priest—Father Bruce Ritter—in an abandoned tenement on New York City's lower east side. In the early years, he was constantly harassed by city bureaucrats. They gradually backed off, however, as the inspiring story of Covenant House became widely known around the city.

My family and I did all kinds of jobs at Covenant House, and over the years I learned some valuable lessons about a world I would otherwise know little about.

I met some of the countless young people from the streets who have never known love and did not know how to accept it. The kingdom of God had never existed for them, until that moment when they walked through the doors of Covenant House. Gradually, they saw a whole new future beckoning to them as they discovered God's love was for them too.

I have also seen God's love through serving as a eucharistic minister at four New York hospitals, including the Cardinal Cooke Health Care Center in Harlem, where I work with the AIDS patients. These people have had tragic lives. Many never knew a mother or father, received limited education, and were brought up on the streets with predictably tragic results—drugs, venereal diseases, jail, AIDS. Essentially, what I do is spend time with these people who are on the doorstep of death.

I try to comfort and console them and let them know that a friend is by their side. I give them water I have brought back from Lourdes and rosary beads blessed there. Quite often they are overjoyed and cry as I pour the blessed Lourdes water on their frail bodies. And of course, I pray with them and for them, asking that the Lord will manifest his love to them through me, whether through my words, my touch, or my smile.

I want these broken, suffering people to feel that special peace that comes from knowing that where they are going, they will find something infinitely better than the pain and grief of the troubled world they leave behind.

I also offer them the Holy Eucharist, the body of Christ. The peace that these people, young and old, find in prayer and communion can be more healing and sustaining than all the medicines the world can provide. I have personally witnessed the miracles that happen as a result of this work.

Many are the times I have walked out of a hospital room with tears in my eyes. I find myself wondering how I could possibly have given the sick half of what they have given to me.

One such occasion occurred at the Cardinal Cooke Health Care Center with a man named Eddie, a man in his early forties who had contracted AIDS, lost over half his body weight, and was now too weak to move. His legs were the circumference of my wrist, and he would weep as I poured Lourdes water on his emaciated body.

Over a period of two years Eddie became a good friend, and I was able to help reconcile him with his wife and a child he had never seen. His wife had been bitter about his disease and had not seen him in two years. Perhaps the good Lord kept him alive longer than his prognosis would have indicated so that this reconciliation could take place.

Once, after giving him communion, Eddie looked at me and said, "Bill, would you please do me a favor? I can't move over myself, and I don't like to ask the wonderful people here to move me too often, because I know how busy they are and I know they feel a little uncomfortable touching my body with all its sores." He went on to ask me if I would very carefully put my arms under his body and slide him over because lying in the same position was extremely painful.

As I looked into the eyes of that dying young man, I was certain that I was looking right into the eyes of Jesus Christ himself. And, as I pulled him over as gently as I could, I said, "Eddie, how about me asking you for a favor? When you get up to heaven and you're sitting at the feet of Jesus and the blessed Mother, would you throw me down a rope and pull me up with you?" And Eddie said, "You got it, Bill." How, indeed, could I ever give as much to people like Eddie as they have given to me?

No matter where I am, whether it is Cardinal Cooke in Harlem or Cottage Hospital in Santa Barbara or Sloan-Kettering Memorial Hospital in New York, I feel so blessed to be able to administer the Holy Eucharist to the sick and dying. In these moments, I am reminded of how limited we are to heal and how limitless we are to comfort. Indeed, enormous barriers are broken by touch, words, and prayer, and I am deeply grateful to be a witness to these great miracles.

The Service of Faith in the Public Square

I have found that infinitely more important than sharing one's material wealth is sharing the wealth of our time and our talents—our energy, our compassion and commitment, and above all, our love.

Yes, writing checks for charities is necessary and important. Through the foundation I created some thirty years ago I have given away many millions of dollars to some very worthy organizations. I plan to give away almost everything I have before I go to be with our Lord.

We all agree that giving money is important. But I can assure you that receiving an impersonal check cannot compare in importance to personal acts of charity. The sight of a human face willing to smile and a human voice lifted up in prayer on behalf of someone in need—such gifts are of incomparable value.

So, yes, it is good to donate money for a new hospital—absolutely. But even better is walking into that hospital after it is built and praying with a cancer patient.

It is good to write a check to support a home for runaway teenagers. But even better is showing up at that home on Saturday morning to serve breakfast to those unloved street kids.

It is great to give money to support a prison ministry. But, did you ever think about going into a prison to teach an inmate how to read and write—or how to pray?

This is the vision of compassion we need to share with our brothers and sisters in the church. And it is the vision we must do our utmost to bring back into the public square.

Tocqueville's biblical fragrance, while certainly diminished, is due for a revival in America as we enter the new millennium. More and more, we are hearing about people of faith who have not forgotten the true meaning of compassion: to "suffer along with" those whom they help. When they do, they are not just only helping "the least of these," they are giving witness to God's power. They are changing lives in ways that no government agency dispensing "entitlements" could ever hope to do. And their numbers are growing day by day.

Let me tell you about two of the most remarkable experiences I have ever had in my life.

Not long ago Chuck Colson, the head of Prison Fellowship Ministries and a friend from the days we both served in the Nixon administration, took me on a visit to a couple of Texas prisons. At one prison, called Jester II, Chuck and I met an inmate named Ron Flowers, who had been through one of Prison Fellowship's intensive accountability programs. Until he went through this program,

Ron had never acknowledged committing the murder for which he had been sentenced. The victim's mother had vowed that he would never get out of prison as long as she lived.

But after going through this faith-based program, Ron did confess to the murder. And incredibly, the victim's mother forgave him.

I happened to be there the day Ron and this woman reconciled. I was standing three feet away when this mother walked up to Ron and hugged him. There was not a dry eye in the room. It was absolutely unreal. She later helped get Ron's sentence commuted.

Could a government program have achieved this kind of healing? Not on your life.

Chuck also took me to a death row prison in Huntsville, Texas. It is called Ellis Unit, and it is the biggest death row prison in the world. Some 450 condemned live there. It was an incredible day, and one that I will never forget. As I walked through the cellblocks, stopping at each individual cell, I prayed with convicted murderers who were just days away from meeting their Maker. I knelt on the steel floor and put my hands through the bars. They knelt on the other side. I gave them rosary beads, I poured Lourdes water on their heads, and I gave them Holy Communion. As I did so, many began to cry. One held on to me and would not let me go.

I intend to return with Chuck whenever I can, because this was one of the most satisfying experiences I have ever had. I truly felt that in ministering to these prisoners, I was doing the Lord's work.

Living Our Faith

Too often today we hear people telling us that the government must stay over here, and religion must stay over there, and never the twain shall meet. But Washington and Jefferson and Franklin and Adams and Lincoln were right. This country will not survive without God. Our nation will not survive unless we reweave, strand by strand, faith-based love and charity with school, government, and every element of society. Separation of church and state—yes, but restrictions on religion—absolutely not.

Some sixteen-hundred years ago, Saint Augustine said that those who follow God have a dual citizenship: They are citizens of both the heavenly kingdom and an earthly kingdom. Because they are inspired by heaven, Augustine said, they should strive to be the best citizens here on earth.

In solving our society's most pressing problems, people of faith bring the commitment and compassion to do the job in a way no one else can.

Living our faith is not a sometime thing that comes easily. It requires us to work at it, to buckle down and renew our commitment each and every day.

To anyone here who might be considering making a new commitment of his or her own, let me leave you with these thoughts.

Not everyone is able to go into the prisons or minister to AIDS patients. But everyone can do something, and there is so much need in the world. Whether you choose to become a eucharistic minister or pursue another avenue of charity, you can be sure of this: You will reap far more than you will sow.

But please, don't wait. Remember the words recorded in St. Luke: "To whom much is given, much is expected."[11] And I would ask: To whom has God given more than to Americans fortunate to be living at this time?

In the midst of all of our abundance, living our faith and answering God's call are the most important goals we could have. Each of us can play a part—to take our vows to serve the sick, the poor, and the forgotten as a personal commitment.

This is the true meaning of fulfilling our duties as people of faith—and as citizens of the freest and most prosperous nation ever known to man.

Notes

1. G. K. Chesterton, *What's Wrong with the World* (San Francisco, Calif.: Ignatius Press, 1994), 37.

2. Adolfo Pesquera, "State Decides to Close Drug Treatment Center," *San Antonio Express News*, 1 July 1995.

3. Byron R. Johnson, David B. Carson, and Timothy G. Pitts. "Religious Programming, Institutional Adjustment, and Recidivism Among Former Inmates in Prison Fellowship Programs," *Justice Quarterly*, 14, no. 1 (1997): 145-66.

4. John McCaslin, "Inside the Beltway," *The Washington Times*, 29 October 1992, A6 or Kate DeSmet, "Church's Newsletter, A Student's Secret Prayer," *The Detroit News*, 7 May 1993, B3.

5. John Adams, *The Works of John Adams, Second President of the United States*, Vol. IX, ed. Charles Francess Adams (Boston: Little Brown and Company, 1854), 299, to the officers of the First Brigade of the Third Division of the Militia of Massachusetts on October 11, 1798.

6. *Basic Writings of George Washington*, ed. Saxe Commins (New York: Random House, 1948), 637.

7. Benjamin Franklin quoted in *Debates in the State Conventions*, Vol. V, ed. Jonathan Elliot (Philadelphia: Lippincott Press, 1941), 253.

8. Quoted in *The Life and Writings of Abraham Lincoln*, ed. Philip Van Doren Stern (New York: Modern Library, 1942), 753.

9. Van Doren Stern, *Life and Writings of Lincoln*.

10. Quoted in *Abraham Lincoln: His Speeches and Writings*, ed. Roy P. Basler (New York: World Publishing Co., 1946), 793.

11. Luke 12:48.

Index

Contributors

Eloise Anderson

As director of the Program for the American Family at the Claremont Institute, Eloise Anderson leads the development of policy approaches related to welfare, education, employment, and health. She was director of the Wisconsin State Department of Health and Social Services until 1992, when she was tapped to lead California's burgeoning Department of Social Services, embracing the nation's largest welfare system and one-fourth of all funds spent nationally on welfare.

Degreed in sociology from Central State University in Ohio, Anderson has completed graduate work at the University of Wisconsin, Marquette University, and the executive program at Harvard's John F. Kennedy School of Government. As one of the most respected and sought-after public welfare officials in America, she has been featured on *60 Minutes*, the *NBC Nightly News* with Tom Brokaw, and the *Jim Lehrer News Hour* on PBS.

John J. DiIulio Jr.

President George W. Bush selected John DiIulio Jr. to lead his newly formed Office of Faith-Based and Community Initiatives. Previously, as director of The Jeremiah Project, he studied and assisted faith-based programs for inner-city youth and young adults, with a special emphasis on programs that focus on achieving literacy, avoiding violence, and accessing jobs. He also served as a professor of politics and public affairs at Princeton University. In Philadelphia he was senior counsel to Public/Private Ventures and in Washington, D. C., was founding director of the Brookings Institution's Center for Public Management.

The author, coauthor, and editor of a dozen books, he is the recipient of numerous awards and has chaired the American Political Science Association's standing committee on professional ethics. In addition to papers in scholarly journals, his articles have appeared in the *Wall Street Journal*, the *Washington Post*, the *New York Times*, *The New Republic*, the *National Review*, the *Washington Monthly*, and *Commentary*; he is also a contributing editor at *The Weekly Standard*.

Jean Bethke Elshtain

Jean Bethke Elshtain is the Laura Spelman Rockefeller Professor of Social and Political Ethics at the University of Chicago and a fellow of the American Academy of Arts and Sciences. A political philosopher whose task has been to show the connections between our political and our ethical convictions, she earned her undergraduate degree from Colorado State University, where she went on to earn her M.A. in history as a Woodrow Wilson Fellow. She received her doctorate in politics from Brandeis University and, as the first female holder of an endowed professorship at Vanderbilt University, received the Ellen Gregg Ingalls Award, the highest award for undergraduate teaching at Vanderbilt. She is the author of more than four-hundred essays in scholarly journals and journals of civic opinion and some 175 book reviews. She also writes a regular column for *The New Republic.* Her most recent books are *Who Are We? Critical Reflections and Hopeful Possibilities* and *Women and War: With a New Epilogue.*

Patrick Fagan

The William FitzGerald Research Fellow in Family and Culture Issues at the Heritage Foundation, Patrick Fagan writes and publishes extensively on social problems such as crime, welfare, child abuse, and drug addiction—and how they relate to the breakdown of marriage. He is the former president of the American Family Financial Association Institute, a nonprofit research and education foundation focused on national economic policy related to family finances.

Fagan served as senior vice president for social policy for the Free Congress Foundation from 1984 and in 1989 joined the staff of Senator Dan Coats. Soon thereafter he joined the Bush administration as deputy assistant secretary for family and community policy in the Department of Health and Human Services.

Born and educated in Ireland, Fagan earned a bachelor's degree in sociology and a graduate degree and license in psychology from University College in Dublin. He completed additional doctoral studies in clinical psychology at American University. He led two community psychiatry teams and trained and supervised physicians from McGill Medical School in family therapy and community building in Canada.

Steve Forbes

Steve Forbes is the president and chief executive officer of Forbes, editor-in-chief of *Forbes* magazine, and chairman of the company's American Heritage division. A widely respected economic prognosticator, he has appeared on many national news programs, including the *MacNeil/Lehrer News Hour, The Nightly Business Report,* and *Wall Street Week.* Forbes is the only four-time winner of the prestigious Crystal Owl Award, which is bestowed upon the financial journalist whose economic forecasts for the coming year prove most accurate. A 1996 and 2000 presidential candidate, he campaigned for tax reform, medical savings accounts, a new Social Security system for younger people, parental control of schools, and term limits. In 1996 he became honorary chairman of Americans for Hope, Growth, and Opportunity, a grassroots issues advocacy organization founded to advance pro-growth, pro-freedom, and pro-family issues. Forbes earned a bachelor's degree in history from Princeton University in 1970 and is the author of several books including *A New Birth of Freedom: Vision for America*, *New York by the Numbers: State and City in Perpetual Crisis*, and *The Right Time the Right Place*.

Douglas W. Kmiec

Douglas W. Kmiec is dean and St. Thomas More professor of law at The Catholic University of America in Washington D. C., as well as the distinguished policy fellow at the School of Public Policy at Pepperdine University. Previously, he held the Caruso Family Chair in Law at the Pepperdine University School of Law. One of America's best-known legal scholars and commentators, Kmiec taught constitutional law for nearly two decades at the University of Notre Dame before joining Pepperdine. At Notre Dame he also directed the Center on Law and Government. He served President Ronald Reagan as a deputy assistant attorney general and was a White House Fellow and two-time Distinguished Service Award winner. He also has lectured in Asia as a Fulbright Distinguished Scholar. Kimec's scholarly research spans both legal and nonlegal areas, ranging from the Constitution to the organization of American society. He writes a regular column for the *Chicago Tribune*, and his books include the provocative *Cease-Fire on the Family* (Crisis Books/Notre Dame, 1995) and *The Attorney General's Lawyer* (Praeger, 1992).

Stephen V. Monsma

Stephen V. Monsma is a professor of political science and former chairman of the social science division at Pepperdine University. He also teaches the course, Religion and Public Policy, in the Pepperdine School of Public Policy. A graduate of Calvin College, he earned an M.A. from Georgetown University and a Ph.D. from Michigan State University. He served in the Michigan House of Representatives from 1972-78 and Michigan Senate from 1978-82. He also has been a member of the Michigan Natural Resources Commission and part of the top management team in the Michigan Department of Social Services. He is the author of many books, including *The Challenge of Pluralism: Church and State in Five Democracies*, *When Sacred and Secular Mix: Religious Non-profit Organizations and Public Money*, and *Positive Neutrality: Letting Religious Freedom Ring*. In addition, he has contributed chapters to numerous books and journals. He has been selected as the lead researcher on a major multi-year study of faith-based welfare-to-work programs in Los Angeles, Philadelphia, New York, Chicago, and Boston.

Michael Novak

Theologian, author, and former U.S. ambassador to the U.N. Human Rights Commission, Michael Novak currently holds the George Frederick Jewett Chair in Religion and Public Policy at the American Enterprise Institute. Perhaps no one has had a more profound impact on the contemporary philosophy and theology and the relationship between religion and economics.

In addition to twenty-five influential books and syndicated columns in *Forbes* and *National Review*, his essays have been published in dozens of periodicals. Novak's seminal works have included *The Open Church*; *Belief and Unbelief*; *The Unmeltable Ethnics*; and *The Spirit of Democratic, Capitalism* which has been printed in every major western language as well as Korean, Japanese, and Bengali. It was published underground in Poland in 1984 and recently in Czechoslovakia, Germany, China, and Hungary.

Novak has taught at Harvard, SUNY, Syracuse University, Notre Dame, and Stanford where, two out of his three years, he was voted one of the two most influential professors by the senior class.

Jack Scott

Jack Scott, senator from the twenty-first district of California, is also Distinguished Professor of Higher Education at Pepperdine University. Scott was elected to the California legislature after serving eight years as president of Pasadena City College, the third largest community college in the nation. He previously served as provost at Pepperdine University and as president of Orange Coast College, Cypress College, and the Association of California Community Colleges Administrators. He received his bachelor's degree from Abilene Christian University, a master of divinity from Yale, and his Ph.D. degree in American history from Claremont Graduate School. His book on John Witherspoon, one of the signers of the Declaration of Independence, was published by the University of Delaware Press in 1982. His articles have appeared widely in newspapers and national magazines. Scott received an honorary doctorate from Pepperdine University in 1991. In 1993 he received the Harry Muttimer Award, given annually to two distinguished administrators in California community colleges.

William E. Simon Sr.

William E. Simon Sr. achieved legendary success in American business, public affairs, and government. After service in the U.S. Army, he graduated from Lafayette College and began his career with Union Securities. He later joined Salomon Brothers, where he was a member of the Executive Committee.

He served as secretary of the treasury under both Presidents Nixon and Ford, where he received the Alexander Hamilton Award, the Treasury Department's highest honor. He was also honored by the Collar of the Republic/Order of the Nile, presented to him in Cairo by President Anwar Sadat, and the Blessed Hyacinth Cormier Award for outstanding Catholic leadership.

Following government service, Simon cofounded several successful companies, including Wesray Corporation, a pioneer in mergers and acquisitions, and William E. Simon & Sons, a global merchant bank.

Simon served on the boards of more than thirty companies, and the Graduate School of Management at the University of Rochester was named the William E. Simon Graduate School of Business Administration in 1986.

An active member of the U.S. Olympic Committee for more than thirty years, he served as its president for the four-year period that included the 1984 games in Sarajevo and Los Angeles and was inducted into the U.S. Olympic Hall of Fame.

Simon was a man of strong faith who considered serving others a God-given responsibility. A eucharistic minister to patients at four hospitals, he made a personal commitment to serve the sick and poor. He created hundreds of scholarships for underprivileged students at both the high school and college levels. He endowed centers, chairs, and professorships at numerous institutions of higher learning and received more than twenty honorary degrees.

Until his death in June 2000, Simon served as president of the John M. Olin Foundation. He was the author of two best-selling books, *A Time for Truth* (1977) and *A Time for Action* (1980).

Charles Van Eaton

Charles Van Eaton is a professor of public policy at Pepperdine University School of Public Policy. Previously he held the McCabe/UPS Chair in Economics at Hillsdale College, where he served as chairman of the Economics and Business Division for nineteen years. During his tenure as chairman, he helped to develop an economics curriculum with an emphasis on the work of Frederich Hayek and Ludwig von Mises, two of the world's most important economists. His recent work has focused on the privatization of government services. A prolific author, he has written more than nine-hundred columns and his writings have appeared in approximately two-hundred newspapers nationwide. His numerous published works include "Revitalizing the American City: A Market Perspective for Detroit" (Heartland Institute), "Privatization: Theory and Practice for Michigan," and "Jail Overcrowding: A Public Problem with a Private Solution?" In addition to his Ph.D. in economics completed at Tulane University, he was trained in biblical studies at Freed-Hardeman University and Harding University and has served as a minister in the Churches of Christ.

James R. Wilburn

James R. Wilburn serves as the founding dean of Pepperdine University's newly formed School of Public Policy. He also is a professor of strategy in Pepperdine's Graziadio School of Business and Management, where he was dean for twelve years. Wilburn received his Ph.D. in economic history from the University of California, Los Angeles, his undergraduate and master's degrees in biblical studies from Abilene Christian University, a master's in history from Midwestern State University, and an M.B.A. from Pepperdine's Presidential/Key Executive program. The author of several books on American history, business management, and leadership, he is the recipient of the McGarvey Award for American History and of the George Washington Medal of Honor from the Freedoms Foundation of Valley Forge. In 1985 he established, with Baron Edmond de Rothschild, the annual Conference on International Strategic Alliances in Geneva and was invited to address the European Parliament. Most recently, at the request of the Yeltsin government, Wilburn has served as cochairman of the U.S. Committee to Assist Russian Reform. He was appointed by President Ronald Reagan to be president of the board of the Citizens for the Republic Education Foundation and serves as corporate director of several companies in the United States and Europe.

James Q. Wilson

James Q. Wilson is the Ronald Reagan Professor of Public Policy at Pepperdine University. Following service in the United States Navy and academic degrees at Redlands University (A.B.) and the University of Chicago (Ph.D.), he began a long and storied career in the public policy arena. From 1961 to 1987 he taught political science at Harvard University, where he was the Shattuck Professor of Government. He subsequently taught at the UCLA Graduate School of Management from 1985 until 1997 where he was the James Collins Professor of Management and Public Policy. A prolific writer, he is the author or coauthor of fourteen books, the most recent of which are *Moral Judgment* and *Moral Sense*. Others include *American Government*, one of the most widely used textbooks in the nation; *Bureaucracy*; and a recent collection of writings, *On Character: Essays by James Q. Wilson.*

Wilson has served several U.S. presidents on national commissions and task forces on crime, drug abuse, and foreign intelligence. He currently serves as chairman of the Board of Academic Advisors of the American Electric System, is on the boards of State Farm Mutual Insurance Company and Protection One, and is a trustee of the RAND Corporation.

In 1990 the American Political Science Association presented him the James Madison Award for a career of distinguished scholarship, and in 1991-1992 he served as that association's president. An elected member of the American Academy of Arts and Sciences and the American Philosophical Society, Wilson has received honorary degrees from seven universities, his most recent from Harvard and Pepperdine University.

Alan Wolfe

A professor of political science and director of the Center for Religion in American Public Life at Boston College, Alan Wolfe is the author or editor of nearly a dozen books on subjects related to the middle class and public morality. His most recent books are *Moral Freedom: The Search for Virtue in a World of Choice* and *One Nation, After All*. He is the recipient of three grants from the National Endowment for the Humanities for his summer seminars for college teachers on "Morality and Society."

Featured in *Who's Who in the East* and *Who's Who in the World*, Wolfe is on the academic advisory board of the National Marriage Project and the Family Studies Institute of Duquesne University. He is also a member of the Lilly Foundation Seminar on Religion and Higher Education.

Wolfe is a consulting editor of *The New Republic* and the *Wilson Quarterly* and writes often for those publications as well as for *Commonweal*, the *New York Times*, *Harper's*, the *Washington Post*, and other periodicals. He served as an advisor to President Clinton in preparation for his January 1995 State of the Union address. Lecturing widely at American and European universities, Wolfe has also been a Fulbright Professor of American Studies at the University of Copenhagen.